My Friend Tom

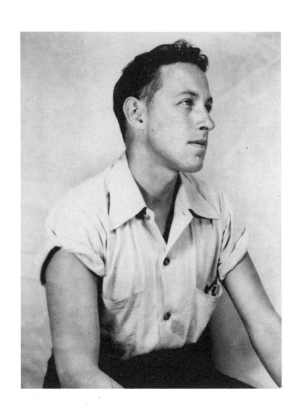

My Friend Tom

The Poet-Playwright
Tennessee Williams

William Jay Smith

Foreword by Suzanne Marrs

University Press of Mississippi   Jackson

www.upress.state.ms.us

The University Press of Mississippi is a member
of the Association of American University Presses.

First printing 2012

∞

Library of Congress Cataloging-in-Publication Data
Smith, William Jay, 1918-
  My friend Tom : the poet-playwright Tennessee Williams / William Jay Smith ; foreword
by Suzanne Marrs.
     p. cm.
  Includes bibliographical references.
  ISBN 978-1-61703-175-5 (cloth : alk. paper) — ISBN 978-1-61703-176-2 (ebook) 1.
Williams, Tennessee, 1911–1983—Criticism and interpretation. 2. Williams, Tennessee,
1911–1983—Friends and associates. 3. Smith, William Jay, 1918-—Friends and associates. I.
Title.
  PS3545.I5365Z8355 2012
  812'.54—dc23
  [B]   2011031697

British Library Cataloging-in-Publication Data available

To Thomas Keith

Bind us in time, O Seasons clear, and awe.
O minstrel galleons of Carib fire,
Bequeath us to no earthly shore until
Is answered in the vortex of our grave
The seal's wide spindrift gaze toward paradise.

—Hart Crane

Contents

Foreword

My Friend Bill: The Poet-Memoirist William Jay Smith

On my desk at home, beside my computer screen, sits a beautifully printed poem that William Jay Smith and his wife, Sonja, sent as their 2007 Christmas card. Titled "Prelude," the poem reads:

> All that I see must in my sight become
> So sparkling clear that waves of vision break
> Upon my eye as on some coral-comb
> The wild Pacific . . . and I summon Blake
> To guide my thoughts beyond that curling foam
> As he would lambs to pasture by a lake
> And leave them frolicking till Kingdom Come.
> And all that now is ill will then be well,
> will then be well;
> And all that now is ill will then be well.[1]

Each day this poem, Bill's poem, cheers me and makes me vividly aware that my friend Bill Smith is a genius. The elegant use of rhyme and meter, the allusion to Keats and invocation of Blake, the artful repetition in the poem's conclusion—all combine to reassure readers that the "sparkling clear" images of poetry will endure, inspire, and bless their lives.

Just as Bill's meditative poem "Prelude" delights me, his humorous poems have delighted generations of children and parents. Witness these lines from "The Floor and the Ceiling":

Winter and summer, whatever the weather,
The Floor and the Ceiling were happy together
In a quaint little house on the outskirts of town
With the Floor looking up and the Ceiling looking down.

. . .

On a screened-in porch in early spring
They would sit at the player piano and sing.
When the Floor cried in French, *"Ah, je vous adore!"*
The Ceiling replied, "You adorable Floor!"[2]

But affirmation and humor have not been the only notes sounded in Bill's poetry. His sequence of poems titled *The Cherokee Lottery* hauntingly reminds us of the removal of Cherokees, Choctaws, and other Native Americans from their land in the southeast to what is now the state of Oklahoma. In one of these poems, "The Pumpkin Field," Bill adopts the persona of a nineteenth-century U.S. Army lieutenant who sees a magnificent and handsome people destroyed by the journey he must enforce. When an Arkansas farmer offers the starving Cherokees, now "skeletal automatons," the pumpkins in his field, they fall upon them until seeds emerge "foaming from their hungry mouths." The lieutenant is left with a nightmare vision of their anguish and his own guilt:

"What have we done to these people?"
    I cried out . . . And then a silence fell;
across the dark I saw
    row after row of pumpkins carved and slit,
their crooked eyes
    and pointed teeth all candle-lit within,
not pumpkins but death's-heads they were
    with features of the vacant
hungry faces I had seen,
    stretching to infinity

and glowing in the dark—

and glowing still when I awoke—

as they do now, and as they always will.[3]

William Jay Smith's poems always will have a powerful impact, moving us from trails of tears in one book to gales of laughter in another, appealing to readers from the ages of five to ninety-five. Of course, Bill's work as a poet has long been recognized and praised. From 1968 to 1970 he was consultant in poetry to the Library of Congress, a position we now more fittingly call poet laureate in tribute to the eminence of those awarded the post. In 1980 Dana Gioia, the poet who would later become chairman of the National Endowment for the Arts, extolled the "clarity, grace, and overt musicality" of Bill's poems and labeled Bill himself as "the master of the short formal lyric." In 1998 Elizabeth Frank, the Pulitzer Prize–winning biographer of poet Louise Bogan, asserted that Bill's poems were "cause for celebration, homage, and gratitude." And in 2000 critic Harold Bloom concluded that "William Jay Smith has been one of our best poets for more than sixty years, and *The Cherokee Lottery* is his masterwork: taut, harrowing, eloquent, and profoundly memorable."[4]

"One of our best poets," Bill Smith is also an astute critic who has shared and continues to share memories of writers who were and are his contemporaries. He has broken bread, laughed, talked shop with many other of our nation's most respected authors—Elizabeth Bishop, Louise Bogan, Allen Tate, Robert Penn Warren, Eudora Welty, Richard Wilbur, and Tennessee Williams among them. Bill has preserved his correspondence with these and other literary figures (his alma mater Washington University has opened this archive for research), and he has also provided us with reflections about his contemporaries. His essay on Louise Bogan tells us much about her passion for poetry and the joy she took from it. Both emotions delightfully emerge from his account of playing *bouts rimés* with Bogan: in this game of rhymed ends, they "would choose the end words, the rhyme scheme, and then as quickly as possible, each produce a poem."[5] In his essay "Eudora Welty and Mushrooms," Bill shows us a playful Welty wittily mocking academic pretensions, and in his interviews with me as I worked on a Welty biography, he provided crucial information about the two men who were the great loves of her life.[6] Similarly, when Lyle Leverich and Donald Spoto were in the process of writing biographies of Williams, Bill provided key insights into his life and work through an essay he had written for the *Dictionary of Literary Biography Documentary Series* and through personal recollections in a memoir titled *Army Brat*.[7] Now he presents us with a full-length memoir of his friendship with Williams, a memoir in which he draws upon his talents as a memoirist and as a poet.

Above all, *My Friend Tom* allows us to know Thomas Lanier Williams, to experience his youthful shyness and madcap humor, his devotion to poetry and drama, his moments of despair, and his Southern gentlemanly manners, which periodically were on display. We learn that as a collegian he was "very, very quiet and soft-spoken," in contrast to his mother with her "maddeningly unstoppable voice." Bill adds, "Once he got to know someone he would let himself go, but otherwise he was quite withdrawn. His stony-faced silence often put people off; he appeared uninterested in what was going on around him, never joining in the quick give-and-take of a conversation but rather listening carefully and taking it all in. He would sit quietly in a gathering for long periods of time until suddenly like a volcano erupting he would burst out with a high cackle and then with resounding and uncontrollable laughter." The side of Tom given to uncontrollable laughter, Bill tells us, was also the side that prompted him to give his briefly owned roadster the name "'Scatterbolt' because you could always hear it before you saw it."

Humor notwithstanding, Bill makes clear that from his youth Williams was devoted to poetry and drama and that poetry would sustain him when his career as a dramatist seemed threatened. The two friends were together in 1940, for instance, when the Boston opening of *Battle of Angels* fell victim to "a terrible blunder" during a simulated onstage fire. Williams himself recalled that "when it came time for the store to burn down it was like the burning of Rome. Great sulfurous billows rolled chokingly onto the stage and coiled over the foot-lights."[8] He felt that his first major production was doomed. Bill feared that his friend might even commit suicide that night and dared not leave him alone at his hotel. Then Tom, in his despair, turned to poetry for solace:

> He went at once to a suitcase and took out a rather hefty anthology of poetry that looked like a library book. . . .
>
> He handed [it] to me and asked me to read to him the poems of John Donne, which I did for the next hour and a half. Why had he chosen Donne rather than Hart Crane or D. H. Lawrence to whom *Battle of Angels* was dedicated? . . . [H]e may have been thinking of what William Butler Yeats wrote to Herbert Grierson about the latter's edition of Donne: "Poems I could not understand or could vaguely understand are now clear and I notice that the more precise and learned the thought the greater the beauty, the passion; the intricacy and subtleties of his imagination are the lengths and depths of the furrow made by his passion. His pedantry and his obscenity—the rock and loam of his Eden—but make us the more certain that one who is but a man like us has seen God." Tom was sorely in need of that kind of vision on that dark night.

It seems only appropriate that Bill, having shared this desperate evening, also witnessed moments of great triumph for Tom. One that he recounts took place late in Williams's life when he received the Presidential Medal of Freedom from President Jimmy Carter. Williams, especially when under the influence of drugs or alcohol, had not always behaved well when receiving accolades. Eudora Welty felt that "poor T. Williams . . . [had] seemed simply unreal" when he accepted the 1969 Gold Medal for Drama from the National Institute of Arts and Letters, but eleven years later at the White House Williams, according to his agent, was "chipper and courtly" and behaved "like the gentleman of the world."[9] Bill, who had come to the ceremony as the guest of Welty, was delighted and proud to see not one but three old friends—Eudora, Tom, and Robert Penn Warren—receiving their nation's highest civilian award.

My Friend Tom thus truly gives us a sense of Tennessee Williams as a person, not a celebrity or an icon, but it does more. It also provides a valuable history of six Williams plays in performance— sometimes Bill reports on opening nights, sometimes on preview performances, sometimes on amateur productions, and once on a transfer to the London stage. Whatever the venue, he discusses the actors, the staging, the reception of *Candles to the Sun*, *Battle of Angels*, *The Glass Menagerie*, *A Streetcar Named Desire*, *Cat on a Hot Tin Roof*, and *Clothes for a Summer Hotel*. Not able to be present for the opening of *The Glass Menagerie* because he was still on active duty in the U.S. Navy, he saw it a year later still on Broadway and by chance encountered the author as they both left the theater. Bill recalls telling Tom that he had been staggered by the magnificence of Laurette Taylor in the role of Amanda. Tom, in turn, told Bill that

> he had come again to see the production because he had
> received reports that Julie Haydon, portraying the sister around
> whom the play revolves, had been over-acting and upsetting the
> play's delicate balance. He had found this to be true, although,
> overwhelmed by Laurette Taylor's performance, I hadn't
> noticed anything of the sort. Julie Haydon, with her emaciated
> beauty and a facial expression bordering on ecstasy, seemed
> perfect in the role of Laura for to the character's physical

infirmity she brought toward the end of the play a suggestion of oncoming madness. But in Chicago, Laurette Taylor had become annoyed by the adulation that Haydon showed her during curtain calls and had pushed her aside when she first tried to kiss Taylor's hand and then stooped to kiss her skirt. It may have been antics of this sort that Tom had now detected but that had escaped me.

Bill himself was disappointed by the performance of Vivien Leigh as Blanche when he saw a London production of *A Streetcar Named Desire* that had been directed by Lawrence Olivier, and he regrets not having seen Marlon Brando and Jessica Tandy, whose performances under the direction of Elia Kazan he felt must have been truer to the play's magnificent script. Eudora Welty, Bill notes, had not liked even Kazan's Broadway version, but Bill adds that Welty did admire *Cat on a Hot Tin Roof*. He includes Welty's program notes for a 1959 Jackson, Mississippi, production of *Cat* and places them next to Williams's own comments about the play—a marvelous juxtaposition.

Compelling as these portraits of performance history prove, even more compelling is the poet William Jay Smith's discussion of Williams's plays as poetry. "Tennessee Williams was first and foremost a poet," Bill writes and then proceeds to establish the truth of this observation. He devotes an entire chapter to Williams as poet, lyric and dramatic, and he discusses the influence of poets—from Shakespeare, Hart Crane, and D. H. Lawrence to Sidney Lanier, Edna St. Vincent Millay, Sara Teasdale, and Vachel Lindsay—on Williams. Then, in separate chapters focused on Williams's plays, Bill contends that these dramatic pieces demand the sort of close reading of image and metaphor that poetry receives. Bill gives *Candles to the Sun* (1937), Williams's first full-length play, just this sort of reading: "If taken literally as a chronicle of social protest, the play can never be fully understood. It must be read as a closely unified and carefully developed metaphor. It is an extended study of light and dark, both inside and outside the characters and the setting. The action moves, as does the sonnet, 'Singer of Darkness,' from dark into light, with all the degrees of chiaroscuro and shadow along the way." Bill believes that Tom's play *Battle of Angels* (1940) utilizes stagecraft for the sensory imagery essential to the play's text: "The playwright wants us to feel exactly what it was like in the small town that he remembers from his boyhood, and so he brings all the senses into play, every sight and sound is called up: we hear drum beats and gun shots, follow thunder and lightning, wind and rain, listen to pinball machines and guitars playing, and catch the constant barking of 'hound-dawgs' tracking fugitives through the woods." And Bill finds *Clothes for a Summer Hotel*, Williams's last play presented on Broadway, to be one of his "most poetic" and "most Shakespearean." In this play, Bill writes, "The characters are indeed ghosts who move on and off stage as they do in Shakespeare, occupying a different time and place and on occasion a different character. . . . This is the most objective of Tennessee's plays but at the same time the most personal. From beginning to end it is all metaphor: as spectators we are in the barred world of madness, a world that sits upon a windy hilltop so that it may receive fully the free-moving and omnipresent, unimpeded spirit of poetry."

Perhaps, we might well conclude, the best interpreter of a poet-playwright's life and work is a poet, especially if that poet is William Jay Smith. Bill Smith invites us into the life of his friend Tennessee Williams. He allows us to share private and revealing moments that can illuminate Williams's work, and he opens our eyes to the metaphoric and sensory dimensions of that work. We, whose literary heritage has been made richer by Bill Smith's poetry, now can have our understanding of a preeminent playwright enriched by Bill's poetic memoir, *My Friend Tom*. Read and enjoy and reflect.

Suzanne Marrs

Preface

This is not a long book but it has been long in the making. When my friend Tom (Thomas Lanier Williams) became immediately famous in 1945 as Tennessee Williams with the phenomenal success of *The Glass Menagerie*, he regularly gave my name to reporters, editors, theater and film critics, biographers, teachers—to anyone anywhere who was, he thought, seriously interested in learning about the beginning of his extraordinary career. For more than half a century I have been responding to questions of every sort put to me by people of every sort from every corner of the world concerning the early years of the great American dramatist who was completely unknown when we first met at Washington University in St. Louis seventy-five years ago.

Tennessee Williams spent his first seven years in Mississippi, but for the rest of his life Missouri and the city of St. Louis, where he now lies buried, were for the most part, physically or imaginatively, his residence. I was a close associate of his there from 1935 to 1940 when we were both students; I, a freshman, and he, a senior, at Washington University, and where he produced his first two full-length plays. Poet Clark Mills, also a university senior, and I met with the poet-playwright Tom frequently, as often as three times a week, at his house on Pershing Avenue a few blocks from the campus. We read our poems to one another, feeling as true poets do, that poetry must be heard before it can be committed to the page. And when not reading, in his living room, I looked and listened and thus got to know Tom well and became familiar with all the sights and sounds that he confronted every day and night in that household he depicted so forcefully in *The Glass Menagerie* and to which, in his imagination, he returned throughout his life in the other plays, poems, and stories he created. I remember his indomitable mother, Edwina, ushering us like some contented, commanding Confederate general into an antebellum mansion with the honey-coated steady monotonous and maddeningly unstoppable voice that Laurette Taylor, in the character of Amanda Wingfield, caught perfectly. The madness in her speech that extended out over the entire household she dominated was echoed from time to time in her talented son's dark down-home Delta drawl when, cut by the cool blade of gallows humor, it erupted in uncontrollable laughter that resounded along the shelves on either side of the fireplace and shook dust from the books they contained. I carry with me the vision of the lonely lovely forever-lost sister Rose drifting in from the shadows, her shrill persecuted voice ruffling the air and rippling her beaded blouse, as she flees the determined drumbeat of the heavy stylishly footed hard-drinking salesman father, Cornelius. Up behind him marches the skinny uniformed little busy-body brother Dakin back from his ROTC training session in the field house of the University.

I want to record the continuing presence in my mind of Tom's family members who appear, in one form or another, in almost all his work, and of his two early influential friends, Clark Mills, the poet, and Willard Holland, the actor and director of the theatrical troupe that presented his plays, and the female members of our Poetry Club who turned up in them. I wish to call back the riverfront of St. Louis as it then was during the Great Depression with the Hooverville shacks on the edge of the Mississippi there below Eads Bridge, as important to Tom as Brooklyn Bridge had been to Hart Crane, and to provide some sense of the entire fog-bound, polluted city that he examined so carefully and to which he gave literary permanence.

In one of my poems I have spoken of life as "neither nightmare nor dream but dream and reality converging," and it is this artistic convergence and all the interacting shifts of light and dark accompanying it that I have followed, early and late, in the best work of my friend Tom (Tennessee Williams) that I attempt here in some rewarding way to explore.

My Friend Tom

Prologue

On November 8, 2009, Tennessee Williams was inducted into the Poets' Corner at the Cathedral of Saint John the Divine, New York, New York, at a Vesper Service at 4:00 p.m. On that day a tribute to him and selections of his work were read by the poet-in-residence, Charles Martin, and some of the electors who had chosen the first poet-playwright to be so honored. A stone was unveiled in the alcove of the cathedral inscribed with Williams's line, "For time is the longest distance between two places," from his play *The Glass Menagerie*. Among Williams's predecessors were Herman Melville, Walt Whitman, Emily Dickinson, Robert Frost, Mark Twain, Ralph Waldo Emerson, Langston Hughes, David Thoreau, Ernest Hemingway, and Louise Bogan.

The Poets' Corner was created in 1984 to memorialize American writers and was modeled after a similar alcove at Westminster Abbey in London. It is administered by a poet-in-residence at the cathedral who serves for four years, and he or she names the thirteen literary electors who join in choosing the writer to be inducted. I was the second of these poets-in-residence, having served from 1988 until 1992, and hence was delighted to be asked to take part in the celebration of the life's work of my friend at the cathedral at 7:00 p.m. on Thursday, November 5, 2009. The participants, in addition to the poet-in-residence, Charles Martin, included Eli Wallach and Anne Jackson, Vanessa Redgrave, Marian Seldes, John Guare, Olympia Dukakis, John Patrick Shanley, Gregory Mosher, Sylvia Miles, Lenya Rideout, Jeremy Lawrence, Wyatt Prunty, Thomas Keith, and Mitch Douglas. David Kaplan, curator of the Provincetown Tennessee Williams Theater Festival, and Thomas Keith, the

New Directions editor, were responsible for assembling this group, all the members of which had either worked with or been inspired by the poet-playwright.

On the death of Tennessee Williams in 1983, James Laughlin, the publisher of his poems and plays throughout his life, said how much he valued what his friend had offered to the world. He recalled that Williams, first and foremost a poet himself, had carried with him wherever he went a copy of the poems of Hart Crane and that he had always been generous to his writer friends, "though you wouldn't hear that from him."

I had been one of his earliest writer friends at Washington University in St. Louis. I had been with him in 1935 when he first discovered the poems of Hart Crane, and he had always been extremely generous to me. After he died, I found in his *Notebooks* the following entry for December 11, 1939:

> Went over to Bill's room at W. U. Dorm. We wrote, I on a new one act which is rather feverishly, desperately flashy. Bill prepared his group for the Poetry Club. Some of his stuff is surprisingly good—he gets nice musical effects and good images—but comes down frightfully in some lines without realizing it at all—still, Bill is a very nice kid and I hope will make some kind remarks over my grave.[1]

The one-act play on which Tom was working was apparently *At Liberty*, the story of Gloria La Greene, an unsuccessful actress who returns home to her mother in Blue Mountain, Mississippi. Gloria arrives, wanton and wasted by consumption, but clings to the illusion that her luck will change and she will be cast for "a marvelous Broadway production." The group of poems that I was preparing no doubt included the short lyric "He Will Not Hear," which the poet Witter Bynner, pleased by my musical effects, awarded first place for an annual prize when it appeared later that year in *College Verse*.

Since Tom died, I have spent many happy hours preparing a long series of kind remarks that I am pleased to be able to make over his grave in 2011 in celebration of the centenary of his birth. Before I begin to set them down in these pages, I should first give my reader some sense of where I came from and what I might have brought with me to St. Louis.

Like Tom, I was a displaced Southerner, born in 1918 in Winnfield, Louisiana, on my grandfather's farm. Of Scotch-Irish and French descent, he had come by ox cart from Georgia, had served in the Louisiana militia during the Civil War, and for that service was later made postmaster of the town of Winnfield. He also opened a general store and edited the only local newspaper. He died when I was three years old, but whatever talent I have as a writer, I believe I inherited from him. My father, unable to cope with farming, enlisted in the army in 1918 as a clarinet player in the band and was transferred three years later to Jefferson Barracks, Missouri, just south of St. Louis on the banks of the Mississippi. It was there with my beautiful Southern part-Choctaw mother and my brother, a year and half younger than I and as different from me as Tom's young brother Dakin was from him, that I grew up between the two world wars with only occasional visits back to Louisiana, where I thought I belonged. This unusual boyhood I have recorded in detail in my autobiography, *Army Brat*, published in 1980. My father, like Tom's, was an alcoholic and a compulsive gambler. As with Cornelius, Tom's father, alcohol and poker got him into serious trouble. Because of drinking on duty, my father remained for years a corporal; and my mother, as a seamstress who made clothes for the officers' wives, kept the wolf from the door. The children from the Barracks were transported by army trucks to St. Louis schools; and because the city then had one of the finest school systems in the country, I benefited, as Tom did, from a St. Louis education and from excellent teachers who encouraged me and my writing. When I won a scholarship to Washington University, where I met Tom in 1935, I had already begun to publish poems in national magazines. At the time of my high school graduation, my father was found drunk on duty and chose, rather than remain imprisoned in the Barracks, to transfer to Hawaii, where he was at the time the Japanese attacked. My mother remained behind, took a job at the Barracks, and divorced my father on his return.

Like Tom I would not have made my way through school without the help of my strong mother, but although my father was difficult and abusive, I discovered in the end that, as a writer, I owed him and his Louisiana family a great deal, just as Tom did to Cornelius and his Tennessee antecedents.

1

Thomas Lanier Williams, Washington University

"Have I told you," Tennessee Williams asks in his *Memoirs*, "that at Washington University we had a little poetry club? It contained only three male members. The rest were girls, pretty, with families who owned elegant houses in the county."[1]

The three male members were Clark Mills McBurney, who, as Clark Mills, was already nationally known as one of the country's most promising poets, Tom (then Thomas Lanier Williams), and I.

One day during my freshman year I read a notice on a bulletin board at the university about a meeting of the College Poetry Society, to which any interested students were invited. It was to be held at the house of Professor Alexander "Sandy" Buchan of the English Department. When I looked carefully at the address, my eyes almost fell out. Professor Buchan lived on Telegraph Road about a mile from the west gate of Jefferson Barracks, where I lived, very far from the University. There were no streetlights anywhere along Telegraph Road during those days, and the numbers on the houses were rarely in evidence. I allowed myself ample time, and after a struggle down the dark road, up treacherous driveways, past fierce watchdogs, I found the house and within it a group of friendly young people who were discussing all that I cared most about. The group consisted mainly of bright and pretty girls who all seemed to know one another and who spoke quickly and knowledgeably of many modern writers I had never heard of. They deferred to a young man, older than most of them, who spoke with great authority; he was Clark Mills McBurney. Tall, with sandy hair and an open and friendly manner, he punctuated his sentences with a chuckle that seemed to come from deep within. Several of his poems had been published in *College Verse*, a publication of the College Poetry Society, edited by Ann Winslow from the University of Wyoming.

Professor Winslow (her real name was Grubbs), with a passion for poetry and what appeared to be inexhaustible energy, must have written hundreds of letters every day to campuses around the country and had organized the College Poetry Society at twenty or thirty major colleges and universities. She raised money for prizes and enlisted the help of established poets to serve as judges for the magazine's annual contests. She had just edited an anthology of selections from *College Verse* entitled *Trial Balances*. The work of a number of undergraduate poets was presented, accompanied in each case by a critical assessment of it by a well-known poet. Here Clark's poems were presented with an essay by R. P. Blackmur; Marianne Moore commented on the poems of Elizabeth Bishop. There were other contributions by Theodore Roethke, Josephine Miles, Ben Belitt, and many others who were just beginning to publish. I bought the book immediately, and it became my introduction to modern poetry. And then —urged on by Clark—I started to read T. S. Eliot and the young English poets, Auden, Spender, Day-Lewis, and MacNeice.

Clark became my mentor and I his adoring pupil. He was then a senior at Washington University and his field was French. I had been placed in an upper section of French Composition. Delighted to learn that there were classes taught by native Frenchmen, I joined the class of Professor Albert Salvan, who afterward taught at West Point and still later became chairman of the French Department at Brown University. In the class, conducted in French, we were reading *Le Grand Meaulnes* (*The Wanderer*) by Alain-Fournier, which I thoroughly enjoyed.

As an assignment early in the semester we were given a list of topics, suggested by the novel, on which we were asked to write. I chose the topic "Silence." When our papers were returned a few days later, I noticed that mine was not among those that Professor Salvan distributed. The next moment I realized that he was holding it in his hand and reading it to the class. At the end of his reading he pronounced my composition of great merit and worthy of a talented French writer, all the more extraordinary to have come from a young American student. He took my essay to Professor Harcourt Brown, who had just come to Washington University as head of the French Department, and Professor Brown soon called me to his office. He questioned me about my background and my plans for the future and asked in which courses I was enrolled. I explained that in addition to English, French, and science, I had enrolled in courses in education, since these were required for a teacher's certificate. High school teaching appeared to be the best I could hope for on graduation. He urged me—commanded me—to drop the education courses at once and to sign up for courses in French literature, which he gave me special permission to enter.

The following week I enrolled in a senior course with Professor Salvan and, with my new friend Clark Mills McBurney and others, was soon reading Marcel Proust in the original. It was shortly afterward that Clark introduced me to Thomas Lanier Williams, who had just registered at the University as a special student, already having spent three years at the University of Missouri intending to continue toward a degree in journalism; but his father, Cornelius Coffin Williams (C. C.), a veteran of the Spanish-American War, horrified that Tom had flunked ROTC, brought him back to St. Louis in 1932 to work in the shoe factory where he was a sales manager.

Before turning to Tom as he was in 1935 with the Poetry Club at Washington University, let us first examine his intervening years in high school in St. Louis and at the University of Missouri.

Tom had been writing constantly since the age of twelve. He had been encouraged by his teachers at Ben Blewitt Junior High and later at Soldan High School. In the summer of 1928 he went with his grandfather, the Reverend Mr. Dakin, to shepherd a group of Episcopalians on a grand tour of Europe. When he returned, he transferred to the University City Public High School for his final semester (his parents had moved to an apartment at 6254 Enright Avenue in the suburb of University City, their ninth move during their first dozen years in the St. Louis area). He wrote an account of his travels for the school paper and it was serialized in several issues. Just before embarking on his journey Tom had written a short story called "The Vengeance of Nitocris," which was published in *Weird Tales* and for which he had received thirty-five dollars. Based on a paragraph of Herodotus, it tells of an Egyptian queen who avenges her father's murder by locking up his murderers in an underground chamber that she floods, drowning them all, while festivities take place overhead. After that, knowing she is doomed, she goes into a smoke-filled room and suffocates herself. The piece opens thus: "Hushed were the streets of many-peopled Thebes."

In 1928, before graduating from high school, Tom spent some months immersed in reading a biography of Shelley and was "fascinated that the poet had been wild, passionate, and dissolute." There had been several women in the life of "Mad Shelley"—Harriett, Mary, and Claire—and thus far only one in Tom's life, the girl he had written to from Paris "with a heart full of love." This was Hazel Kramer, a lovely red-haired girl he had known since she was twelve and he was fourteen and they had grown close, dating, dancing, and going to the movies together. When she graduated in 1929 with her best friend Esmeralda Mayes from Mary Institute, the fashionable St. Louis school for girls, they both had planned to go to the University of Missouri, where Tom's parents had decided to send him. Hazel's grandfather was persuaded, perhaps by Tom's father, to see that Hazel went instead to the University of Wisconsin to keep the young couple apart. When Tom arrived at the University of Missouri, his first letter was to Hazel proposing marriage. She replied that they were too young to think of any such thing. He thought of her for years afterward but the romance was over, and long after she had married Terrence McCabe, whom she had met at the University of Wisconsin, Tom told his mother that the beautiful little red-head had been "the deepest love of his life."

On October 29, 1929, just one month after Tom registered at the University of Missouri at Columbia, then a pretty small college town midway between St. Louis and Kansas City, the stock market crashed. The headline in the show-business weekly, *Variety*, put it succinctly: "WALL ST. LAYS AN EGG." "The most dramatic event in the financial history of America," the paper said, "is the collapse of the New York Stock Market. The stage was Wall Street but the onlookers covered the country. Estimates are that 20 million people were in the market at the time." The word was soon all over the campus, and Tom wondered if he might have to join many other well-to-do students throughout the country who were having to drop out of universities. But to his amazement, his father, Cornelius, not only allowed Tom to remain, but expressed his great satisfaction on hearing that the young man had accepted the pledge to the fraternity Alpha Tau Omega, even though it would cost him more each month. He had prevailed on a pair of young cousins in the ATO at the University of Tennessee to notify the Columbia Chapter that "the son of an executive in the International Shoe Company was hiding out in a boarding house and this would not do, since he was descended from the Williamses and the Seviers of East Tennessee, was a published writer and a traveller of the world."

Shortly after Tom's arrival on campus a local paper ran an interview headed, "Shy Freshman Writes Romantic Love Tales for Many Magazines." It reported that Tom, who planned to enter the School of Journalism, had had a "number" of stories published in *Weird Tales* and *Smart Set* magazines and had received twenty-five dollars for an article based on the shy freshman's "own unhappy marital experiences." Tom had already learned that reporters, like dramatists, tend to exaggerate. The description of him, however, was precise and accurate:

It bothers Mr. Williams to have anyone ask him questions about himself. He is little more than five feet tall. He has clean-cut features, and smooth brown hair. His eyes, which have a look that seems thousands of miles away, add to the unapproachable and reserved appearance which he presents. He is equally as reticent and shy as he appears and feels that having his stories published is nothing out of the ordinary.

The article also said that he admitted that his inspiration for his stories rose not so much from actual experience as "from reading a wide variety of authors," including his favorite writer, Louis Bromfield.

What the article did not say was how much he disliked having attention called to his small stature. This was true for the rest of his life. It didn't help to have it pointed out that Keats, like many other great writers, was not very tall.

As for the young poet's emotional development at the University of Missouri, Lyle Leverich has summed up the situation: While undeniably Tom was experiencing growing attraction to members of his own sex, it was evident in the journals he began to keep several years later that even then he could not understand this in himself. Like many another sensitive youth, particularly with strong religious and societal restraints, he refused to give quarter to feelings he would only come to comprehend and accept in time. For most of his three years at the university, Tom was troubled by the problem of sexual identity, his homoerotic impulses countered by a strong sensual response to girls, who were constantly in his company. He had come to the borderline of a new terrain of love but would be unable to cross it for years.

In April 1930 Tom entered his one-act play *Beauty Is the Word* in the annual Dramatic Arts Club contest sponsored by Professor Ramsay of the English Department and it won a sixth-place honorable mention. Set in the South Pacific, the play concerns a missionary and his wife with the unlikely names of Abelard and Mabel. Their beautiful niece Esther, reproaching them for their bleak theology, says: "Fear and God are the most utterly incompatible things under the sun. Fear is ugliness. God—at least *my* God—is beauty." Tom was the first freshman to win an honorable mention, but he would have preferred to win the fifty-dollar first prize and a workshop production of his play. In May 1930 Tom's short story, "A Lady's Beaded Bag," appeared in the campus literary magazine, *The Columns*. The story contrasts the attitude of a trash picker who discovers a lady's beaded bag filled with money with that of the owner to whom he returns it. It is ironic that Tom was hoping like the trash picker to receive money for his story, but none was forthcoming, and he could see that only with journalism could he hope to earn money with his writing.

At the end of the school term Tom was nineteen and his grades for the fall semester had been B minus and C plus for the spring, and even with his eighteen absences this made him a better-than-average student. When he returned home for the hot summer, Cornelius told him that he would have to find work to help cover his expenses for the coming year. The only job he could find was selling subscriptions to the *Pictorial Review* for twenty-one dollars a week. Tom finally gave up on magazines and went downtown to enroll in the ten-week course at Rubicam's Business School. His sister Rose would join him and he would help her with the work. His mother, Edwina, explained that they were both selling two shares of stock in their father's shoe factory to pay for the course. Tom soon became an excellent typist, but Rose found it impossible to cope with the workload. Oddly enough, exactly five years later, prior to meeting Tom at Washington University, I had enrolled in the same course at Rubicam's, and midway during the course I received a telephone call from my father, who made an infrequent stop at the Jefferson Barracks Post Office to pick up the mail and found a letter addressed to me, saying that the meeting of students with the judges of the Swope Scholarship established by Gerard Swope of the General Electric Company was taking place later that morning. I was horrified to have to face the judges in my shirt sleeves without a tie or jacket, but I prevailed all the same and won the scholarship, which covered my tuition and all my expenses for four years at Washington University, mainly because of a strong recommendation I had received from General Walter Short, who was then commandant of Jefferson Barracks.

The next year Tom continued his writing, but seemed to neglect plays. He was listed among the fifty contestants for the First Annual Mahan University Essay Contest. The first prize of fifty dollars was won by Harold Vincent Boyle for "Confessions of a Well-Read Man." Boyle went on to become a syndicated columnist and journalist. Tom received honorable mention for his short story "Something by Tolstoy" but was disappointed because with first place he would have had both the top honor and fifty dollars.

"Something by Tolstoy" tells of a Jewish bookstore owner whose Gentile wife deserts him to run away for a career as a singer. Then, years later, recalling the great love she had had for her husband since their childhood, she returns to the store. What she finds is that grief has left him withdrawn and unable to recognize her. "Do you want a book?" he asks. "Yes," she answers, but she can't remember its title and she tells him the story of their own lives and their passion for each other. The storekeeper replies that it sounds familiar to him and thinks that it is "something by Tolstoy." What the story seems to say is that reality is only what has been created by the imagination.

In his third year Tom began his courses in journalism. In October 1931 the Theatre Guild's production of Eugene O'Neill's *Mourning Becomes Electra* starred the famous Russian actress Alla Nazimova, whom Tom and I were to see together five years later on tour in Ibsen's play *Ghosts* at the American Theater in St. Louis. It made such an impression on Tom that he declared at the time that it decided him to write for the theater. There was renewed interest in O'Neill on the campus and a production of *The Hairy Ape* was proposed by Professor Ramsay for the workshop in the spring. The second play that Tom entered in the contest of the Dramatic Arts Club was one called *Hot Milk at Three in the Morning*. It was very similar to O'Neill's one-act play *Before Breakfast*. The play is a depiction of a poor Depression-era "laborer and his whining sick wife." The figure of a man trapped by marriage like a caged animal was one that Tom had encountered in his own father.

The wife says, in the heat of their argument, "You know that before you married me you was just a common tramp, that's all you was!" Angered, he replies:

Yeah, you bet I was. An' I was satisfied, I was happy! You bet I was. I tramped from Massachusetts to Oregon, and I tramped from Oregon to Alaska. An' I stayed one place just as long as I liked it and when I got tired of it I went on to another place. I was free! Yeah, I was a real man then, before I married you. I wasn't afraid of no one. And now what kind of thing have I turned into? A mill hand! A wage slave! A chained animal! An' I work for a little grey weasel that I'd like to tear the guts out of, but I gotta say "Yes, sir" to him, because if I lost my job I couldn't just hit the road again like I used to, and go on to another town and another job, 'cause I got a sick wife and a bawling baby a-hanging on to me. That's what I got when I got hitched up with you!

Tom would later revise *Hot Milk* and rename it *Moony's Kid Don't Cry*, thinking perhaps of O'Neill's *The Dreamy Kid*. Along with two other one-act plays it would win recognition in a contest sponsored by the Group Theater.

In January Tom joined the Missouri Chapter of the College Poetry Society, of which there were twenty-five female members and seven male members. Anyone who knew Tom well would certainly not have made him treasurer, but so they did and he got hold of the society's ledger. The first three pages were given over to 1931–1932 expenditures and receipts with Tom's dues of $2.50 noted and, under expenditures, treasurer's "book and folder, 65 cents." The remainder of the 65-cent book was blank, and in 1936 Tom would put it to more practical use as his own personal journal.

Those who came to the Journalism School expected that they were just going to spend their time writing. They did not realize they would be expected to master a craft and a whole range of newspaper functions. Tom's first assignment was that of reporting the cost of local produce and listing the prices of light and heavy hens, sour cream, eggs, and geese, which left him little time for creative writing. The next beat was even worse because he was told to write an obituary. "Well, I went to the house where the death had occurred," he said later. "There was all this squalling going on, and it was not a pleasant place to be. Quite obviously a death had occurred, I reported that the professor had died, actually, it was his wife who had died, not he. But it came out in the paper that *he* was dead. So they immediately fired me, of course. I couldn't take journalism seriously."

In the same spring of 1932 a tragic event took place about three hundred miles north of Havana, and it would make a great impression on Tom and would remain in his mind for the rest of his life. Aboard the liner *Orizaba* on Wednesday, April 27, just before noon, the poet Hart Crane, returning from a Guggenheim Fellowship in Mexico, came up on deck dressed in pajamas and wearing an overcoat. Henry Allen Moe of the Guggenheim Foundation reports the event as follows: "He walked rapidly aft, threw the coat on the deck, climbed up on the rail and jumped over the side. Life preservers were thrown at once, the ship was maneuvered and a boat put over the side but no trace of Crane was found. He had been seen once after his body struck the water and apparently he made no effort to reach the life preservers thrown to him." Hart Crane would become the poet that Tom revered above all others, and throughout his life it was Tom's wish upon his death to have his body sewn up in a sack and dropped at sea as close as possible to the spot where Crane had jumped.

Tom was only beginning to experience the disappointments and rejections that most writers undergo. His play *Hot Milk at Three in the Morning* took only thirteenth place in the One-Act Play Contest and failed to have a workshop production. There was small solace in that a short story, "Big Black: A Mississippi Idyll," won an honorable mention in fifth place. This story, which was the narrative of a black man on a road gang and his imagined relationship with a white woman, was noted for its dialogue and mature treatment of a controversial subject. It was his final effort to gain recognition for his work at the University of Missouri. He had been praised in a letter from Professor Ramsay that he later quoted: "Your absence at the University has been a matter of real regret to all of us who knew the excellent work you did here in the last few years especially in creative writing." The letter gave him advice about placing the fine story "Big Black."

While employed during the following summers at the International Shoe Company, Tom would work on his verse at odd moments during the week and on Saturday would go downtown to the Mercantile Library, where he would read voraciously all afternoon. On Sunday he would work on completing the short story that he had started during the week. He put much of himself and his distress on losing Hazel Kramer into his story "The Accent of a Coming Foot," based on a poem of Emily Dickinson. Shortly after completing the story he accompanied Rose downtown to the movies at the Loew's State Theater and on the way back home in a service car he became increasingly tense and had the driver stop at Saint Luke's Episcopal Hospital. At the emergency entrance he convinced the hospital employees that he was having a heart attack. Rose called Edwina to say that he had had a stroke, which was not the case. The doctor who examined him said he was underweight and suffering from complete exhaustion. The hospital kept him for nearly a week and as a result Tom was allowed to resign his position at the shoe factory and to enter Washington University as a special student.

Tom wanted very much to go somewhere away from home for the rest of the summer where he could write all the time. His grandmother Dakin came to his rescue by inviting him to Memphis, Tennessee, and it was there that he wrote a play that was produced on July 12, 1935. One of the Dakins' neighbors in Memphis, to which they had just retired, was a young woman named Dorothy Shapiro, who was a member of a local little theater group called the Rose Arbor Players. The play *Cairo, Shanghai, Bombay!* was a "one-act melodrama" and on the title page of the manuscript it is said to be by Dorothy Shapiro and Tom Williams. Tom wrote the principal part of the play, and Dorothy Shapiro the prologue and epilogue. It is set in a seaport town and it was, in four scenes, he said, "a farcical but rather touching little comedy about two sailors on a date with a couple of 'light ladies.'" Tom at the time had clearly seen a good many movies for the cast included Millie, "a coarse affable little girl of the Mae West type"; Chuck, "a sailor who has been around"; a noted author described as "a pretentious young intellectual." Tom recalled with pleasure the laughter, "genuine and loud," at the comedy he had written.

Returning in September 1935 from his summer in Memphis to University City, Tom found himself in a handsome two-story house at 6634 Pershing Avenue that Tom's father had agreed to lease for two years. In a letter to his grandparents, Tom joyously described the new home, a far cry from the dark cluttered apartment on Enright Avenue that had served as the setting of *The Glass Menagerie*:

> The house is perfectly lovely, even prettier than I had expected.
> It is Colonial style throughout. The living-room is gorgeous.
> It has a big crystal chandelier and crystal candelabrums on the
> long white mantal [sic] built-in bookcases on either side of the
> fireplace . . . the most charming small home I've ever seen. We
> found everything in perfect order, the grape arbor loaded with
> ripe grapes and the rose garden in full bloom. The place seems
> so quiet and spacious and dignified after our sordid apartment-

dwelling that it doesn't seem like we are the same people. I'm sure you would be crazy about it if you were here. The street is quiet as the country. But only a half block from the campus and city car-lines.

The house was guarded in the front by two huge oak trees on either side of a well-tended lawn. It became the regular meeting place of the core of our Poetry Club, as Tom called it. I was the kid, the youngest of the group. Tom was seven years older than I, and Clark five. Because he seemed to have read everything that mattered in both French and English, Clark became our mentor.

Well over six feet, Clark seemed even taller because he walked with a buoyancy that made him appear ready to leap forward at any moment to meet any challenge that life might offer. He was not handsome but had ordinary delicate though unremarkable features, a pencil-thin nose and mouth, both set in a fair-skinned face that flushed easily. It was his eyes that were extraordinary, a dull gray-blue that lit up like the underside of a crashing wave when, with a resonant voice and quick bubbling laugh, he gave vent to an unending irrepressible enthusiasm on every subject he attacked.

He introduced us to Laforgue and Apollinaire and held forth at length on T. S. Eliot's *The Waste Land* and on James Joyce's *Ulysses*. Although at this time I understood little about either one, I was sure that with Clark's assistance one day I would.

Clark classified everyone he met according to whether or not he or she had a soul. "He has no *soul*, that guy," he would say emphatically about some blunt insensitive type.

I had never heard anyone outside of church speak of people's souls, but I soon felt as he did that this was the most important of human attributes. Whatever else I had, having been admitted to Clark's little circle, I knew that I had a soul and that alone set me apart from my dull classmates. The soul, of course, was of great importance in the work of Tennessee Williams. The heroine of his play *Summer and Smoke* is Alma Winemiller, who is the soul or smoke of the title—the exponent of something "immaterial—as thin as smoke," as John Buchanan who has known her since childhood, said of her.

Every young woman Clark met was immediately under his charm, and he was the envy of all the other young men who were studying literature or trying to create it. I stayed with him frequently at his house near the University, and in one corner of the sun porch where I slept he had installed an archive of photographs of his conquests past and present. He spoke as if taking these beautiful creatures off to bed had been the easiest and most natural thing in the world. Seize the day indeed he did, and he had a mistress, as all young men, or at least all young French men that I had read about, were intended to have. He wrote poems and stories dedicated to the latest of these and set down in black ink on long legal pads in such careful script that it looked as if they had already been published. Clark had at the time published far more than Tom.

It is hard to believe that the unknown Thomas Lanier Williams would, in ten years, as Tennessee Williams, produce *The Glass Menagerie*, which, with Laurette Taylor in the leading role, would make him famous. When we met in 1935, Tom showed few signs that would point to this extraordinary development. He had received honorable mention for two one-act plays and two short stories at the University of Missouri and had one one-act play performed in Memphis, Tennessee. During the next five years he would be exposed to the two most important influences in his early career—that of Clark Mills, the published poet, and Willard Holland, director of the St. Louis theatrical group, the Mummers. There was evidence of these influences a few months after we met. In October 1936 the Webster Groves Theater Guild staged his one-act play *The Magic Tower*. With Willard Holland and Clark Mills, Tom attended a rehearsal of *The Magic Tower*. "Had a pleasant evening," he wrote. "Met [Director David] Gibson in café. Drank a couple of beers and felt rather desperately gay, recited Ernest Dowson on the way home.

Wet streets and lamps. Disappointed in the play. Too sugary, but I don't feel like doing anything better. I am in one of my defeatist moods about writing if I could only always love my work—then I would be a great artist but I could never be vain." The following night Tom attended the performance of his play with Rose, Edwina, and Dakin. After the curtain came down on *The Magic Tower*, the last of the three new plays to be performed, the judges met to decide the winner and it was Thomas Williams. The *Webster Groves News Times* gave Tom his first enthusiastic review. The play, it said, was "a poignant little tragedy with a touch of warm fantasy. It treats the love of a very young, not too talented, artist and his ex-actress wife, a love which their youthful idealism has translated into a thing of exquisite white beauty. They call the garret in which they live 'The Magic Tower' and are happy there until the artist's belief in his star fails, then The Magic Tower becomes a drab garret once more and tragedy like a gray woman glides in to remain. The play was exquisitely written by its poet author." The writer of this review turned out to be a part-time member of our Poetry Club at the University. This was Anne Jennings, the wife of Blanford Jennings, known to us as B. J., who taught English in the Webster Groves High School. Anne Jennings was herself an actress. Clark said that she looked exactly like the film star Fifi Dorsay and that she always looked as if she were playing a French maid and even if she wasn't she looked as if she ought to be.

When Clark and I arrived on Pershing Avenue for our regular private Poetry Club session, Edwina Williams ushered us from the hallway into what appeared to be the interior of an antebellum mansion. Its living room contained Oriental rugs, silver, and comfortable, if not luxurious, furniture. The house was in an affluent neighborhood and was higher on the social ladder than Clark Mills's modest house in Clayton. Our entire brick bungalow on Telegraph Road to the west of Jefferson Barracks would have fitted comfortably into one or two of its rooms.

Clark and I usually sat on a sofa against the wall to the left as we entered the living room and Tom sat facing us in a large blue overstuffed chair, which years later he described in an essay:

This overstuffed chair, I don't remember just when we got it. I suspect it was in the furnished apartment that we took when we first came to Saint Louis. To take the apartment we had to buy the furniture that was in it, and through this circumstance we acquired a number of pieces of furniture that would be intriguing to set designers of films about lower-middle-class life. Some of these pieces have been gradually weeded out through successive changes of address, but my father was never willing to part with the overstuffed chair. It really doesn't look like it could be removed. It seems too fat to get through a doorway. Its color was originally blue, plain blue, but time has altered the blue to something sadder than blue, as if it had absorbed in its fabric and stuffing all the sorrows and anxieties of our family life and these emotions had become its stuffing and its pigmentation (if chairs can be said to have a pigmentation). It doesn't really seem like a chair, though. It seems more like a fat, silent person, not silent by choice but simply unable to speak because if it spoke it would not get through a sentence without bursting into a self-pitying wail.

Over this chair still stands another veteran piece of furniture, a floor lamp that must have come with it. It rises from its round metal base on the floor to half a foot higher than a tall man sitting. Then it curves over his head one of the most ludicrous things a man has ever sat under, a sort of Chineseylooking silk lamp shade with fringe about it, so that it suggests a weeping willow. Which is presumably weeping for the occupant of the chair.

It was perhaps not clear to Tom at the time that by always taking his father's chair he was in a real sense assuming the direction of our literary gathering. If it was Clark who set the tone of our activity, it was Tom who gave it the energy that it needed desperately to move ahead.

"I could never have imagined anyone writing as he did," Clark recalled. "He would do, say, a half page or two pages, and it was fast—he was fast on the typewriter—he would be operating as if blindly. He was never sure if he knew where he was going but when he got there—when he finished that passage and it might not be right—he'd toss it aside and start all over again. While he would do the whole business over, it would go in a different direction. It was as if he was throwing dice—as if he was working toward a combination or some kind of result that wouldn't have *any* idea what the right result might be but would recognize it when he got there. You know, usually one sits down and writes page one, two, three, four, and so on—but he would write and rewrite and even in the middle of a passage he'd start over again and slant it another way."

Clark told us how from an early age books had been a part of his life, although his father, like Tom's, thought that "book learning" was a waste of time. At the age of eleven Clark had become interested in Aldous Huxley and took the streetcar down town to the main public library and tried to check out Huxley's *Antic Hay.*

"It was Clark who warned me," Tom said, "of the existence of people like Hart Crane and Rimbaud and Rilke, and my deep and sustained admiration for Clark's writing gently but firmly removed my attention from the obvious to the purer voices in poetry. About this time I acquired my copy of Hart Crane's collected poems, which I began to read with gradual comprehension."

"What I remember," Clark said, "was the impact Hart Crane had on him. That struck him like lightning. I was amazed by his reaction. I was impressed by Crane; I thought he was pretty damned good but I didn't regard him as highly as Tom did. He just went haywire over him."

Clark seemed always happy to start talking and ready to go on at length. But Tom was, at the time, one of the shyest men I'd ever known, very, very quiet and soft-spoken. Once he got to know someone he would let himself go, but otherwise he was quite withdrawn. His stony-faced silence often put people off; he appeared uninterested in what was going on around him, never joining in the quick give-and-take of a conversation but rather listening carefully and taking it all in. He would sit quietly in a gathering for long periods of time until suddenly like a volcano erupting he would burst out with a high cackle and then with resounding and uncontrollable laughter. Tom's mother, Edwina, who always graciously greeted us, was a busy little woman who never stopped talking, although there wasn't much inflection or warmth in the steady flow of her speech. One topic, no matter how trivial, received the same emphasis as the next, which might be utterly tragic. I had the impression, listening to her, that the words she pronounced were like the red balls in a game of Chinese checkers, all suddenly released and clicking quickly and aimlessly about the board.

"Of the pretty girls who provided lovely refreshments and décor for our Poetry Club," Tom wrote later in his *Memoirs*, "I remembered only the name Betty Chapin and the first name of another, the wealthiest, Louise, who took us all out in the family limousine to a ballet performance one night."

Tom got the name wrong. His friend was Betty Chapell, whom he had met in an evening class on the short story taught by Professor Frank Webster. Betty was working on a novel and he spent many hours at her house, which was not far from his, helping her with it. When *The Glass Menagerie* appeared, Betty was convinced that Tom had taken the idea of turning Rose into a cripple from the memory of her crippled sister.

It was Louise Krause who took us to the ballet performance, or it may have been both Helen Longmire and Louise Krause. In any case, their friend Mary Guggenheim arrived with the ballet from Washington or New York and had tickets for all of us. Most of these girls, who were Jewish, made their débuts at the annual St. Louis

Veiled Prophet's Ball. Helen Longmire, who was tiny and dark with the long face and dark eyes of Nefertiti, was one of the most loyal members. We gathered regularly at her house on Papin Avenue in Webster Groves. The house was particularly memorable because Helen's uncle had spent some time studying painting with the Impressionists in France and there were striking paintings of his on all the walls and there were very thick rugs on which we used to stretch out and listen to Helen's brother play pieces of Mozart or Brahms on the piano. At one of the meetings at Helen's place when we came with bottles of beer someone, running through the hall to the kitchen, accidentally knocked off a vase. This was not, as Tom observed, the last meeting of our Poetry Club. "Something like a riot occurred with one male member chasing a female member round and round a fifty-dollar 'vahse,' which resulted in that ornament's complete demolition." A charming scene but a slightly exaggerated one.

Because Tom was seldom allowed to take the family Studebaker out, I usually provided transportation for our meetings. When I entered the university, at first I drove to the campus in the morning with Jack Glascock, the son of one of the officers at Jefferson Barracks, who also enrolled, but if I stayed on I would have had to take the long streetcar home. A few months later we acquired a Model-A Ford, which we christened "La Cucaracha." Clark and Tom and I would crowd together in La Cucaracha. Months before, Tom had himself acquired a little roadster he drove around. He called it "Scatterbolt" because you could always hear it before you saw it, but by this time you couldn't see it all, it had disappeared. One rainy night we ended up in a ditch in front of Helen's house. We frequently went also to the house of Louise Krause, who Tom is correct in identifying as one of the wealthiest of the group. A graduate of Mills College in California, she had a kind of slanted smile permanently disjointing her face and a steady laugh. She was writing a graduate thesis on the poems of John Donne, and her own work proved to be an inspired copy of his and met with our approval.

One of the most successful gatherings was at my little bungalow on Telegraph Road just outside of Jefferson Barracks. The bungalow had little space—just four rooms—and we had to move one bed out of the front bedroom to make room for the group. My mother was a great hostess in the Southern tradition. Tom loved her at once— with her long auburn hair and dark eyes and bubbling laughter, she was particularly the kind of Southern woman that he immediately took to. They became fast friends and she frequently called him and spoke at length with him whenever he returned to town. I had been immediately drawn to Tom because of his Southern background. I was also a displaced Southerner, having come up at the age of three from my father's family farm in Louisiana. It was back there that I thought I really belonged, especially after we returned for a short visit when I graduated from grade school. For all his life Tom thought of the days of his boyhood in the rectory of his grandparents in Clarksdale, Mississippi, as the happiest of his life, and it was to them he returned constantly in his work. I also felt close to Tom because like him I had a drunken, gambling father. I did not learn until much later of Cornelius's scandalous scene when he was rushed to Barnes Hospital because one of his poker mates had bitten one of his ears off. My father, a compulsive gambler, played poker every payday and came home one night with his pockets stuffed with greenbacks; my mother and I found him sprawled on the floor with his pistol in his hand, with which he had shot up the porch and might well have killed us all. He lay there with the remains of his drunken evening spilling out in front of him on my mother's spotless floor.

Like Tom I also had a younger brother and we were as unlike each other as Tom and Dakin. I did not have a schizophrenic sister like Rose, but there had been mental illness in my family and years later I had a schizophrenic son.

Clark remembered that in those days "Tom was attracted, peculiarly, to very large, fat girls, and in fact, at one party he surprised the whole group. There was a fat girl there, and he didn't say very much to her—actually there was nothing we heard him say to her—except that he went over and sat down beside her and held her hand all evening."

This plump beauty was Frances Vought, about whom I had composed a little verse:

> There was a young lady named Vought
> Whose delight it was to emote.
>   She would say with a tear,
>   "I am not wanted here!"
> Then get up and take off her coat.

Clark said that Tom came to his house with "a piece he had written—it was a kind of prose poem rather than a short story—and in it was a very, very fat wife of the owner of a plantation. And the foreman was an *exact* duplicate of Tom himself physically, just absolutely perfectly. She was sitting on a porch swing and swinging back and forth, and he was standing near her with a black snake whip, one that you snap. Her refrain was, 'God, ain't it hot? God, Jesus, ain't it hot?' His refrain was, 'Let's go inside where it's cool and quiet,' and then, snap, the whip would go at her heels and she jumped. And this went on over and over again, and finally it led up to the line where Tom and I simply collapsed with laughter. Picture Tom reading, 'Oh, c'mon—I love you 'cause you're as big as America' and her replying, 'All right, I'll go in, but you must promise me, you won't hurt me.' Well, we just fell on the floor laughing—the picture of this enormous fat woman and little skinny Tom—because in those days he was very thin and small." (This, of course, became a scene in the play *27 Wagons Full of Cotton* and in the film script of *Baby Doll*.)

Clark Mills was certainly the most important influence of this time on Tom Williams, but there were others, among them Alice Lippmann and her daughter Margaret Pinkus. Alice Lippmann, the widow of a prominent St. Louis physician, Dr. Gustave Lippmann, had a large impressive Spanish-style house near the University with a large, vaulted living room. In it a painting of a black Madonna that apparently had originated in the Philippines hung above the fireplace. The Madonna, about which the *St. Louis Post-Dispatch* had written an article, had about it an air that pervaded the darkness of the huge room, highlighted by the gold notes of the brass trays in its corners. There were piles of manuscripts that Alice had left on all the little tables and chairs and on the steps leading up to the dining room.

Alice Lippmann was the sort of eccentric who delighted Tom. They had met after they both received poetry prizes in the annual Wednesday Club contest. Alice was a tiny white-haired woman with a boyish bob who had a real passion for poetry. She carried with her a reticule stuffed with old envelopes and torn notebooks on which she had scribbled some lines of verse, and she would turn to whoever happened to be next to her to help her to put those lines together somehow so that she might produce a poem worthy of her talents. She had about her an air of permanent distraction. Once Tom and I went to dinner at her house in the country and we found that she was speaking with great difficulty. "Alice, have you had some extractions?" Tom asked. And then she told him that she had gone for a walk in a field and overcome momentarily by a fit of depression she had cried, "Dash it all!" and had thrown aside all her manuscripts and with them her false teeth, which she had then been unable to find. Alice Lippmann was not really able to bring her own poetry into focus, but she had the greatest appreciation of the poetry of anyone she met who showed any real talent. So she turned her attention in every way she could to Clark, Tom, and me. She provided a link with the great outside literary world which she wanted us to join once we had escaped from the backwater of St. Louis. She had entertained well-known writers when they passed through the city, among them, Harriet Monroe, the editor of *Poetry* magazine, and Edgar Lee Masters, the author of *Spoon River*.

Help with Tom's plays and his poems came from Alice Lippman's daughter Margaret, the wife of Lothar Pinkus, a science teacher at a St. Louis high school. Margaret had a background in science but she also had read widely in modern literature and had an acute critical mind. She was able to see what was right in our poems and she gave us clear and sound advice on how to remedy what was wrong. She was also an effective critic of the plays that Tom had then begun to concentrate on.

A year after we met, Clark left on a fellowship to spend two years at the Sorbonne in Paris. As soon as he left, we all waited anxiously for his letters that detailed, in that careful black script of his, his adventures and, as I gathered, reading between the lines, his continuing conquests. No one waited more eagerly for those letters than his current love, Frances Van Meter, a tall dark-haired willowy creature who looked, wherever she happened to be, as if she had just risen, naked and fine-boned, from a *déjeuner sur l'herbe*. She always had one or more of Clark's letters in her hand when she joined us for lunch at the Art School Cafeteria, the walls of which were covered by the latest awkward and oppressive nude studies executed by current art students. Francie would read us long segments of the letters, looking distractedly from time to time at her wristwatch, which she kept on Paris time so that she would know exactly what Clark was doing at every hour of the day or night. I wasn't at all certain that he was precisely where she pictured him to be. In any case, I was delighted to think of him there, enjoying all the sensuous pleasures that Paris had to offer.

We knew something about Tom's sister Rose, but we rarely saw her when we came to the house. We were aware that she was undergoing treatment for her mental condition, although we did not know, as even Tom himself did not then know, how very serious her condition was and how a few years later she would undergo a prefrontal lobotomy.

On one occasion when his parents were away on a holiday in the Ozarks, Tom invited Clark and me and another friend, Willie Wharton, to share some whiskey with him. Clark had known Wharton at the University and found him amusing. I did not. He had little to say of any interest but he never stopped talking. At the time he was married to Minerva Prim, a former debutante, who stayed at home with their little baby. Wharton would take us up to their apartment and seemed to enjoy having us listen to their uninteresting and interminable arguments. I saw him years later, much subdued and married to a nurse, who appeared to be able to manage him better than Minerva had.

The evening at Tom's, after several drinks, Willie began making obscene telephone calls to people whose names he had picked at random from the phone book. I have a vision in my memory of Rose appearing suddenly on the stairs in a fluffy white dress and, outraged, threatening to tell her parents when they returned about what was happening. This she did to Tom's great distress.

"After she had tattled on my wild party," as the playwright later recounted in his *Memoirs*, "when I was told I could no longer entertain my first group of friends in the house—I went down the stairs as Rose was coming up them. We passed each other on the landing and I turned upon her like a wildcat and hissed at her:

"'I hate the sight of your ugly old face!'

"Wordless, stricken, and crouching, she stood there motionless in a corner of the landing as I rushed on out of the house.

"This was the cruellest thing I have done in my life, I suspect, and one for which I can never properly atone."

Although Mrs. Williams had banned Tom's friends from the house, she tried to organize other social occasions to raise the tone of the family in their new home and to elevate Rose's eligibility.

Roger Moore, a good-looking and brilliant young man, lived across the street from the Williamses and had called to ask Rose to go with him to a Democratic rally, and he seemed in every way exactly the kind of proper gentleman caller that Edwina had been hoping would appear on the scene. "A Rhodes scholar," Lyle Leverich wrote, "he had received his Ph.D. in political science at Yale and was running for mayor of University City, but unfortunately he had pitted himself against a powerful incumbent, a cog in a political machine, and to make matters worse, he tried to use logic and ethics as a rationale to win over the voter. It was like using the blade of a finely honed sword to cut through concrete; to his disillusionment, he was to discover the hard rock of American politics."

Roger took Rose out occasionally, but Tom was much more interested in Roger's sister, the beautiful young poet Virginia Moore, to whom he showed his poems and invited to our poetry gathering. Virginia Moore, who had been married to Louis Untermeyer, had left him after only a few years of marriage and returned to her home in St. Louis with her small son. She had published one or two volumes of poetry, and her work had appeared in Louis Untermeyer's anthology. She was a strikingly beautiful woman, but, along with her beauty, we admired her connections with the literary world. She had met all the important people and was a breath of fresh air from the great outer world. Edwina Williams thought her impressive and found reassurance in her approval of Tom's work. This approval from someone so acceptable socially seemed to make her feel that Tom was doing very well, although I don't think she had any real idea what he was up to. What mattered most to her was that he was at the university and appeared to be on his way to getting a degree.

On May 27, 1937, after losing the election, Roger Moore, who had been placed in the sanatorium where Rose had been, threw himself in front of a truck near the sanatorium. The afternoon of the funeral, Virginia Moore read one of her poems at the funeral service at her home.

We don't know how Roger Moore's death affected Rose, but in any case, her condition continued to deteriorate. The insulin treatments that she had been receiving did her little good. Her sexual fantasies, her obscene language, and her delusions about her father's sexual behavior continued. It was not until January 13, 1943, that a bilateral prefrontal lobotomy, with the consent of Edwina Williams, was performed in St. Louis by Dr. Paul Schrader with Dr. Hoctor assisting. Already in 1937 Tom thought of Rose's eclipse as final, and he contributed this poem to the literary magazine *The Eliot* at Washington University:

Valediction

She went with morning on her lips
down an inscrutable dark way
and we who witnessed her eclipse
have found no word to say.

I think our speechlessness
is not a thing she would approve,
she who was always light of wit
and quick to speak and move—

I think that she would say goodbye
can be no less a lyric word
than any song, than any cry
of greeting we have heard.[2]

Tom continued to write both poems and plays, and I had the rare privilege of attending in St. Louis, on Saturday, March 20, 1937, a performance of *Candles to the Sun*, his first full-length play. The performance took place in the auditorium of the Wednesday Club, an elite women's cultural organization. The play had been produced by an amateur theatrical troupe, the Mummers, and directed by Willard Holland, who played one of the leading roles, and, more importantly, had almost single-handedly helped to shape the final version of the play from the more than four hundred unnumbered typewritten pages of various drafts that now repose at the Harry Ransom Humanities Research Center in Austin, Texas. This was the second of two performances, but the major one, of *Candles to the Sun*, which had had, we learn from the typescript, several other tentative titles, including *The Lamp*, *Place in the Sun*, and *Candles in the Sun*.

The primary focus of the Mummers was drama of social concern, and this play, presenting as it does the travails and struggles of three generations of a family of coal miners in the Red Hills of Alabama, seemed definitely to fit the bill. The play appeared first anywhere in the 2004 edition of New Directions thanks to the fortuitous, wise, and thoughtful intervention of Jane Garett, who played the important role of Star, the wayward daughter of this strict Puritanical coal-mining family, and Dan Isaac, who meticulously edited and reconstructed the Mummers script. It will now delight a worldwide audience of readers, and eventually theatergoers, as it did the perceptive newspaper critics and others in those small, but extremely enthusiastic, gatherings years ago. It was for me not only a decided pleasure, but also an absolute revelation, all the more astonishing because I had come fully prepared, I thought, to give my heart-felt approval to any offering of my dear friend and close associate, Thomas Lanier Williams, however modest and unpolished it proved to be.

Dakin Williams, Tom's younger brother, together with his parents, had attended the Thursday, March 18, premiere (or preview as the Mummers preferred to call it). He remembers that Tom had sat at some distance from his family and from most of the others in the audience, alone in an aisle seat, which he had insisted on having. When to thunderous applause, loud cheers, and resonant footstomping the full cast gathered for numerous curtain calls, they suddenly burst out singing "Solidarity Forever." The celebrated union anthem, totally uncalled for in the script, gave the play an aura of propaganda, which the playwright, despite his pronounced sympathy for victims of social injustice, had clearly not intended.

I knew, of course, that Tom had written plays, any number of short ones, each of which he usually referred to as a "fantasy." But for me at the time he was first and foremost a poet, and it was as a poet that I expected him to make a national name for himself. And indeed he did just that, but not for his poems as such but rather for the poetry of his plays, which was powerfully revealed in Candles to the Sun.

One of Tom's most significant short "fantasy" plays with which I became acquainted was Me, Vashya. In early 1937 Tom eagerly awaited the announcement of the three one-act play winners in the annual contest in English 16, Professor William G. B. Carson's "Technique of Modern Drama." English 16, the only writing course offered at Washington University except for Professor Webster's in the short story, was quite popular on the campus. The students wrote one-act plays and at the end of the year three plays were chosen and given workshop productions. One of the three was selected as the best and its author was awarded fifty dollars, a considerable sum in those days, especially for students. Tom had received a B in the course for the first semester, and after his play *Death of Pierrot* had failed to get even an honorable mention in the contest of the Webster Groves Theatre Guild the previous year, he was hoping he would fare better with Professor Carson. "Horrible if I were eliminated," he wrote in his journal. And horrible indeed it was when that elimination of his play *Me, Vashya* was announced.

I remember his bitterness at the time. The decision was said to have been that of an "independent jury," but Tom thought, as others of us did, that it was solely Professor Carson's, especially when the winner chosen for a full production was a play by Wayne Arnold, who appeared to be Carson's favorite in the class. His play *First Edition* was a drawing-room comedy concerning a recent winner of the Pulitzer Prize. Although not mentioned by name, this was the local author Josephine W. Johnson, whose lyrical novel *Now in November* Tom, Clark, and I very much admired. *First Edition*, a bright little piece, was the absolute opposite of Tom's somber dramatization of the murder of a powerful munitions maker, Vashya Shontine, who sold armaments to both sides in wartime. And war was much on everyone's mind. The assassination the previous summer of the poet-playwright Federico García Lorca by General Franco's Fascists in Spain enraged us all. Tom was attempting to deal with a large and very dark subject, and ironically it was precisely this subject, Professor Carson later revealed, that caused him to eliminate Tom's play. *Me, Vashya* may now seem, as apparently it did when read aloud in

Carson's class, laughably melodramatic, but as the youthful fantastic treatment of a very real problem it was to us, his fellow beginning writers, serious and moving.

What was particularly hurtful to Tom about this defeat was that, while on the surface his subject appeared remote, he had put so much of himself and his own life into this play. Lady Shontine's madness is clearly a reflection of his sister Rose's mental breakdown which so haunted Tom at the time, and the blunt, obsessive vulgarity of Vashya himself surely owed much to that of Tom's alcoholic father, who was making his sister's life and his own totally unbearable.

Tom Williams's next failure was a private rather than a public one. At about the time of Carson's rejection, Tom read to Clark and me the just-completed draft of what was apparently one of his first attempts at poetic drama. It was *Ishtar: A Babylonian Fantasy*. He had first tackled such an exotic subject in 1928 when, at the age of seventeen, he had written a short story, "The Vengeance of Nitocris," that had been published in *Weird Tales*. One would have thought that now at the age of twenty-six Tom would have left behind such attempts at Flaubertian exoticism, but no. Here presented to us in his rich Southern voice was a bit of Babylonian Gothic. This may have been the resurrection of a much earlier piece or a blind stab at verse drama that was then so popular. In any case, he did not get very far in his reading before Clark and I exploded with laughter. Tom responded not by clamming up, mute and hurt, but rather by immediately joining in with his celebrated cackle, astonished himself that he could have seriously set down such patent nonsense.

I found in 2003 only one page remaining of *Ishtar* in the Harry Ransom Humanities Research Center in Austin, Texas. A complete copy of the play has since been discovered there since Tom never discarded anything. I quote from it only these few lines to show how very far Tom had come with the truly spare and moving poetry in every line of *Candles to the Sun*.

Ishtar
(A Babylonian Fantasy)

Ishtar that naked walked
Beyond the seventh gate of Hell for Tammuz sake
Has heard my prayer!
Let us be wanton then! Give me your lips!
Give me your saffron-scented lips . . .
What's this!
Oh, here's a sorry end! My lover sleeps.

And then a few lines further on:

I see the silver arrow of the dawn on the heels of the night.
Hail, Dawn! I salute you!
Hail, rising sun!
Hail Ever-Conquering Worm That Eats All But The Sky!

For a less florid effort, "Sonnets for the Spring," Tom received first prize in a poetry contest at the Wednesday Club. The award was presented to him on his birthday, March 26, 1936, in the same auditorium where *Candles to the Sun* would appear almost exactly a year later. It had been established in 1925 by the celebrated poet Sara Teasdale, whom Tom greatly admired. He was aware that in 1914, after rejecting the proposal of poet Vachel Lindsay, she had married Ernst Filsinger, a highly successful international St. Louis businessman, who made and sold shoes. She divorced him in 1929, and four years later, having found life in St. Louis intolerable, took an overdose of sleeping pills and was found dead in her bathtub. Tom had been very moved by her suicide and had written an ode to her, "Under April Rain."

He turned again to April, that cruellest of months, in his prize-winning sonnets. The first of these, "Singer of Darkness," serves as a fitting prelude to *Candles to the Sun* because it deals, as does the play, with the struggle between light and dark:

Singer of Darkness

I feel the inward rush of spring once more
Breaking upon the unresistant land
And foaming up the dark hibernal shore
As turbulent waves unfurled on turbid sand!
The cataclysm of the uncurled leaf,
The soundless thunder of the burning green
Stuns every field. The sudden war is brief,
And instantly the flag of truce is seen,
The still, white blossom raised upon the bough!
(Singer of darkness, oh, be silent now!
Raise no defense, dare to erect no wall,
But let the living fire, the bright storm fall
With lyric paeans of victory once more
Against your own blindly surrendered shore!)[3]

Reed Hynds, reviewing *Candles to the Sun* for the *St. Louis Star-Times*, contended it was certainly not a propaganda play, as some "lobby critics" had thought, but rather "an earnest and searching examination of a particular social reality set out in human and dramatic terms." In a separate interview in the same paper, Tom had explained that "the candles (in the title of the play) represent the individual lives of the people. The sun represents group consciousness. The play ends as a tragedy for the individuals, for in the end they realize they cannot achieve success and happiness apart from the group but must sacrifice for the common good." I think at the same time that for Tom this had not only a social but also a personal reference. John Donne, a poet whom Tom particularly appreciated, had written, "No man is an island, entire of itself; every man is a piece of the continent, a part of the main," and these lines might well be an epigraph for *Candles to the Sun*. Tom, speaking personally, referred at the time to the "Island of Myself," and it was, he later declared, to "ward off the dread of loneliness that he wrote." If he was an island, he knew that, in his life as in his work, he had to create a bridge to humanity, to a greater world beyond the self.

If taken literally as a chronicle of social protest, the play can never be fully understood. It must be read as a closely unified and carefully developed metaphor. It is an extended study of light and dark, both inside and outside the characters and the setting. The action moves, as does the sonnet "Singer of Darkness," from dark into light, with all the degrees of chiaroscuro and shadow along the way. The two principal pivotal characters are the heroines, Star, the miner Bram Pilcher's daughter, and Fern, his daughter-in-law. Note the careful choice of names, each with its own metaphorical implication. Star moves from her virginal purity that like the real star above her cuts clearly through the camp's darkness, drawn by her own sensuality to the false bright light of Birmingham, the urban dark. She loses her chance to regain that innocence when Red, the spiritual organizer she loves, is murdered. She turns then to the brothel that had always awaited her and from which she will send some of the dark money she earns to help Fern, ironically, purchase freedom from the mine and light for young Luke, her son, whose name means light. Fern, on the other hand, like the plant for which she is named, grows up out of darkness into light: her clean pure self is aware that she can move from her grief and her dark inner self into the blinding, liberating light of the sun. To obtain the greater freedom that the strike provides for the entire community, Fern sacrifices all that she has strived for. The final scene with Fern transcendent in the rocking chair and light streaming through the open door is heart-breaking in its intensity. The intensity is prepared for us by the stage directions of the final scene that are in themselves pure poetry: "*Winter has broken up and it is now one of those clear, tenuous mornings in early spring. A thin, clear sunlight, pale as lemon-water comes through the windowpanes of the cabin which is now barer and cleaner-looking than usual in this strange light."* Heartbreaking also at the same time is Bram, the "Old Man of the Mines" who has preferred to remain in the dark, to go down daily into the dirt to dig his own grave, a mole who knows nothing but the dark and is blinded by sunlight. He moves finally into a deeper level of the dark, into the madness from which there is no return.

It is what Henry James calls "the madness of art" that saves Tom from the madness that he contemplated in his sister and that he so feared would overtake him as well. The ghost of Rose hovers over this entire play, rising from the heavy morning mist that Luke sees, "thick as wood smoke down on the hollow." Fern and Star are both aspects of Tom's imaginative vision of Rose: Fern, evoking her enduring and transcendent innocence; Star, an innocence lost to a destructive sensuality of the powerful sort that he felt had brought on Rose's madness.

Clark has told that he and I attended the Saturday performance of *Candles to the Sun* with the "underground crew" of our rebellious Bohemian confrères. Among them may have been the star members of the League of Artists and Writers whom Tom had met when he attended their weekly meetings in 1936 at the old courthouse near the St. Louis riverfront: poet Orrick Johns, novelist (and Marxist) Jack Conroy, short-story writer J. S. Balch, and humorist Willie Wharton. Whether or not they were all there I am not sure, but I have the distinct recollection that we all went on, along with Tom, to the apartment of Jack Conroy, where we spent the rest of the night with some tough heavy-drinking types I had never before encountered. Clark had this memory of Tom that night:

> He was there at the beginning of the show, but at the intermission Tom was gone—nobody could find him. Finally, I found him outside. It was a cold night—he was sitting on the curbstone in front of the theatre with a bottle of whiskey—and he was drunk as a skunk and in total despair. Apparently,

something had gone wrong, or he imagined it. I know he was intensely concerned with the reaction of audiences, and now suddenly he saw the play as hopeless, and he was drinking himself into oblivion. He refused to go back in—he saw it as just a total disaster. That was the only time I ever saw him really drunk.

I have a feeling, now that I have examined the play carefully and know much more about its author than I did then, that it may not have been something that had gone wrong in the production but that it was simply too painful for him to watch a play in which he had put so much of himself and his sister. Of *The Glass Menagerie* he said late in his life: "It is the saddest play I have ever written. It is full of pain. It is painful for me to see it." To my mind *Candles to the Sun* is also one of Tom's saddest plays, full of pain, but one of the most beautiful. It now deserves a place beside *The Glass Menagerie*.

Tom's direct involvement with the theater at Washington University came in an odd way as an actor in a French-language production put on by the university's French Department. This was *Les Fourberies de Scapin* by Molière, which appeared shortly after *Candles to the Sun*. Mrs. Harcourt Brown, the wife of the French Department chairman, had a passion for the theater and a determination to present French drama, however difficult the casting and however varied the French accents of the actors she rounded up. Edgardo Beascoechea, a Mexican student, Thelma Richardson, and I had acted in one of Mrs. Brown's first efforts, but that was modest beside *Scapin*. We were again enlisted and Tom was persuaded to take the part of the old father. He said afterwards to the Mummers director Willard Holland:

I made my stage debut last week in the Molière. I was not at all nervous, actually enjoyed myself on the stage which surprised me tremendously as I had always fancied myself a hopeless victim of stage fright. Instead of being frightened by the full-house, I was stimulated and found myself adlibbing both lines and action—so now I am a full-fledged thespian.

I had less enthusiasm than he did for his performance. I wrote later:

> He read his French lines with a kind of hound dog ferocity and deliberation as if he were chewing on a large section of the Mississippi Delta. When he moved woodenly across the stage with absolute seriousness pounding the floor with his cane, small and square in his satin suit, and enormous blond wig flopping about his shoulders, he gave a performance that a more sophisticated audience would have taken as high camp. As it was, our local audience had not the remotest idea of when to laugh since it had not a clue as to what was going on.

In her introduction to the New Directions 2001 edition of *Fugitive Kind*, Allean Hale has said of this second full-length play by Tennessee Williams to be produced by the Mummers in 1937:

> It is a veritable index to his later work as he tries out characters, situations, and themes he will develop in plays from as early as *Battle of Angels* (1940) to as late as *The Red Devil Battery Sign* (1975). It is a surprise that, as an apprentice playwright, his source was the movies and more surprising to discover him as a radical writer. The Depression, which forced him to quit college to work in a shoe factory for three years, had politicized him. . . . For once we know the origin of an undiscovered Williams play. In January, 1937, Tom wrote in his journal that he had seen a "lovely" motion picture, Maxwell Anderson's *Winterset*. There were some shots of Brooklyn Bridge that were fairly breathtaking. I can well understand Hart Crane's inspiration by this . . . probably the most exciting piece of architecture in America. Jo Mielziner's set, the soaring expanse of Brooklyn Bridge receding into the fog, became more famous than the play itself.

Inspired by the set and by his favorite poem, Hart Crane's "The Bridge," Tom laid his new play on the St. Louis waterfront near Eads Bridge, itself famous as the first steel bridge in the world. While the bridge is only mentioned in Williams' play as the place of Leo's attempted suicide, it becomes a metaphor for the play itself as a bridge to Williams' future works.[4]

Fugitive Kind is one play on which Clark and Tom may be said to have worked in tandem. Clark recalled a summer day in their "literary factory"; in his "dim cellar," he wrote:

> Each of us on a kitchen chair, your typewriter
> fluent as automatic gunfire, as you sketched
> gestures and intonation, dialogue, behavior,
> and I with index finger, pecked and brooded,
> weighing the sound or color of a word.
> On one St. Louis summer day,
> sweat pouring down on us, we conjured up
> —snow!
> Once, I recall, you thus explored a drama in a flophouse
> while I wrote of a winter white with tons of snow . . .

Many of the words and phrases from Clark's moving poem "The White Winter," which Allean Hale reproduces in her introduction, found themselves in the final speeches of Tom's characters.

Colin McPherson reviewed *Fugitive Kind* in the *St. Louis Post-Dispatch* when it opened in December 1937. He wrote that the play "describes vividly the life in a big city 'flophouse.' Even with the best of acting, *Fugitive Kind* would still be somewhat amateurish and the performance is spotty. Some extraordinary credit should go to the Mummers, however, for giving a local playwright his forum and for attempting to present the life close at hand in the theater." Reed Hynds also reviewed the play in the *St. Louis Star-Times:* "That Thomas Lanier Williams is a playwright to watch was demonstrated again by the Mummers last night when the dramatic group produced his new play, *Fugitive Kind*. While less intense than his *Candles to the Sun*, it is a consistent, vital and absorbing play.... Williams shares some of the faults as well as some of the virtues of the lions of the day (Sidney Howard, Ben Hecht, and Maxwell Anderson) he wants to say something forceful and true about the chaos of modern life. But like them he seems clearer about the way to say it than what to say. His play has theatrical substance, but its thought is confused."

It is ironic that *Fugitive Kind* is one of Tom's plays that his father appreciated, probably because it showed the triumph of the G-man over the criminal, as the Hollywood films of the time usually did. Tom was no doubt thinking of the outcasts, the poor fugitives, on the waterfront there below the building where his father worked, who were the products of the capitalist greed which his own father represented.

The father's presence, which is felt very much throughout the play, is made clear in Tom's later description of the ride he took to work with him every morning in the Studebaker:

> This was a long ride, it took about half an hour, and seemed much longer for neither my father nor I had anything to say to each other during the ride. I remember that I would compose one sentence to deliver to my father, to break just once the intolerable silence that existed between us, as intolerable to him, I suspect, as it was to me. I would start composing this one sentence during breakfast and I would usually deliver it halfway downtown. It was a shockingly uninteresting remark. It was delivered in a shockingly strained voice, a voice that sounded choked. It would be a comment on the traffic or the smog that enveloped the streets. The interesting thing about it was his tone of answer. He would answer the remark as if he understood how hard it was for me to make it. His answer would always be sad and gentle. "Yes, it's awful," he'd say. And he

didn't say it as if it were a response to my remark. He would say it as if it referred to much larger matters than traffic or smog. And looking back on it, now, I feel that he understood my fear of him and forgave me for it, and wished there was some way to break the wall between us. . . .

I often wonder many things about my father now, and understand things about him, such as his anger at life, so much like my own, now that I'm old as he was.

I wonder for instance if he didn't hate or despise "The World's Largest Shoe Company" as much as I did. I wonder if he wouldn't have liked, as much as I did, to climb the stairs to the roof.

I understand that he knew that my mother had made me a sissy, but that I had a chance, bred in his blood and bone, to some day rise above it, as I had to and did.

In the autumn of 1938 after Clark had left for a teaching position in the French Department at Cornell, Tom turned his attention to the creation of what he called the St. Louis Poets' Workshop, which he formed with me and in which we were joined by Louise Krause and Elizabeth Fenwick Phillips, who later married Clark Mills and as Elizabeth Fenwick wrote several fine mystery novels. We had some stationery printed and sent poems to all the leading magazines with a covering letter signed by a fictitious secretary of the workshop. In a few carefully chosen words the letter described the great poetic flowering then taking place in St. Louis. The poems enclosed, the secretary stated, were representative samples of this remarkable Midwestern Renaissance. The editors addressed were less impressed by our flowering than we were: the poems all came back.

With Clark gone, Tom visited his basement where they had held forth with their "literary factory." "On the wall . . . directly before us," he wrote, "was tacked up a little verse of our own composition which was to serve as a grim reminder—as some writers keep skulls in their studies:

For lack of food some writers died
while some committed suicide,
and all though great or small in fame
returned to dust from which they came.

To this Tom now added a credo: "For every artist, experience is
never complete until it has been reproduced in creative work. To
the poet his travels, his adventures, his loves, his indignations are
finally resolved in verse and this in the end becomes his permanent,
indestructible life."

At this important moment in his life, Tom realized that his experience would never be completed and finally reproduced in creative
work until he made a final break with family and with St. Louis.
This he was now prepared to do, and a play contest provided the
incentive. The Group Theatre in New York was offering a five-hun-
dred-dollar prize, and though the age limit for entrants was twenty-
five, Tom decided to send several of his plays for consideration, giving his birth date as 1914 rather than 1911; and furthermore, on his
way to New Orleans, he would mail the plays from the home of his
grandparents in Memphis and he would sign the works "Tennessee
Williams." Although Tom later was fond of ascribing the change to a
Southern weakness for "climbing the family tree" and to his heritage
as a Tennessee pioneer, he really had no idea at the time where the
name had come from and where it would take the person that it
would come to represent.

I knew nothing of the fantastic immediate impact that the city
of New Orleans had on Tom and nothing of his February trip from
New Orleans to Los Angeles with his new musician friend James
Parrott, first by Ford V-8 and then by bicycle, until Tom returned
to St. Louis in early September. He told me then also that a week
before his birthday in March he had received a special one-hundred-
dollar award from the Group Theatre in New York for the plays he
had submitted to their contest and that the Group Theatre had put

him in touch with an agent, Audrey Wood, who was to represent him for almost the entire rest of his life. She placed "The Field of Blue Children" with *Story* magazine, his first publication using the name "Tennessee."

I had moved to the University campus for the fall semester, and when he came to visit me there, Tom brought me a book of poems by Witter Bynner, given to him by the poet in Santa Fe. Tom's visit to Frieda Lawrence in nearby Taos particularly moved him, and he spoke with great enthusiasm of the play that he planned to write based on the "ideas or philosophy" of D. H. Lawrence, whom he admired almost as much as Hart Crane. He came with this poem that he had dedicated to Lawrence:

Cried the Fox
For D.H.L.

I run, cried the Fox, in circles
narrower, narrower still,
across the desperate hollow,
skirting the frantic hill.

And shall till my brush hangs burning
flame at the hunter's door
continue this fatal returning
to places that failed me before!

Then, with his heart breaking nearly,
the lonely passionate bark
the fugitive fox rang out clearly
as bells in the frosty dark,

Across the desperate hollow,
skirting the frantic hill,

calling the pack to follow
a prey that escaped them still.

Taos, 1939[5]

Before Tom left St. Louis again for New York, he made this entry
in his journal:

Sunday—9/16 17/39—End of the St. Louis period—leave
tomorrow midnight for New York. Time here has passed in
a flash. Nothing happened. *Nothing* at *all.* Written practically
nothing & so I don't feel too good. Had hoped—intended—to
go to N.Y. with new play script. But I go almost empty handed
because I want to go somewhere—to get away—the old flight
motive—May God be merciful to me and open some door,
some avenue of escape.

Tom rode to New York in a car driven by Frances Van Meter, who
was taking Clark to Cornell University in Ithaca for his second year
there. In New York he did little more than see a few plays and meet,
for the first time, his agent Audrey Wood. He was back in St. Louis
in early October, where he completed a play he first called *Shadow
of My Passion,* which ultimately became *Battle of Angels.* He took
me to the American Theater to see Tallulah Bankhead playing the
lead in *The Little Foxes.* We went backstage to meet her afterward
and he told me that she had been interested in his new play but that
the director had found someone else. What he did not tell me was
that he had originally written the play with Bankhead in mind, and
in August he had cycled all the way from Provincetown to Dennis
on Cape Cod to see Bankhead, who was acting there in *The Second
Mrs. Tanqueray,* and to leave the script with her. When he returned a
week later, she had said that she was not interested in the role, which
was later taken by Miriam Hopkins. Tom showed me at the same

time the house that his parents had just purchased at 53 Arundel Place, a comfortable light brown, brick Colonial with a garden.

To say that he was eagerly awaiting news of his application for a Rockefeller fellowship would be a great understatement. He was truly desperate now, feeling that this was his last chance ever to make a break from his family and St. Louis. In his journal he wrote:

> Friday, 10 November: I am strangely remote from every-thing—insulated—cut off from the main stream. Home—the attic—the literary life—the creative trance—it makes you feel like you have practically stopped living for a while. I want life and love again—and a swift flow of significant experience. The Rockefeller fellowship? Still no word! I wait. —*J'attends*! Goodnight—let us hope it *is* good.

Over a month later the good news did finally come. I had picked him up to go to a meeting of the Poetry Club. The very next day a congratulatory telegram arrived from Audrey Wood. He spent the afternoon giving the news to the local papers, and that evening he went with Louise Krause and her fiancé, Robert Haas, who was a protégé of Gertrude Stein, to have dinner with Mrs. Lippmann. It was a pleasant evening although the food left much to be desired. Mrs. Lippmann served them pie that was so awful that, Tom said later, "Bob stuffed his in his overcoat pocket." In his journal he noted:

> Dec 28, 1939—Leave for Memphis to see Grand and Grandfa-ther and possibly a little of Mississippi—then N.Y.C.! Week has been full to brim (for *me* social activity)—I've basked in the limelight—an actual celebrity for my little friends here, who have really been very sweet to me, especially Mrs Lippmann and Bill. . . . Full of plum pudding and ready for bed. —*G'night*. (And, Tom, please try to remember not to act like a regular sonovabitch!)

He needn't have added that final admonition—he behaved the next night like an angel when we all gathered around the Christmas tree in Louise Krause's beautiful home in Ladue for what proved to be the announcement of her engagement to Robert Haas as well as a farewell party for Tom. The prothalamium that Gertrude Stein had written specifically for the occasion had been beautifully printed in a pamphlet on pale blue paper and copies of it had been tied with ribbon to the branches of the tree.

Louise asked me to read it aloud, and I was happy to do so:

Prothalamium for Bobolink and His Louisa

> Love like anything
> In war-time
> Day and night
> In peace and war-time
> Birds are Bobolinks
> In war-time
> Girls are Louises
> In war-time

War-time Peace-time. Two in one. In Peace-time.
Two in one and one in two. In War-time. Louise
and Bobolink are one. In Peace-time in War-time
Peace-time.

> They say
> How do you do. And we say,
> How do you do too.
> And they say very well I thank you
> Which pleases them
> And us too
> Two and two that is one is two

THOMAS LANIER WILLIAMS, WASHINGTON UNIVERSITY

Which is you
Louise and Bobolink

Thank you.
They are engaged. To be married.

Gertrude Stein
Bilignin, 1939

The festive evening provided undoubtedly the proper send-off for Louise and Robert and it struck just the right note for the success that finally awaited, we were certain, our poet-playwright friend in New York.

2

Battle of Angels

I had arrived early at the Wilbur Theatre in Boston for the opening
of *Battle of Angels* by Tennessee Williams on December 30, 1940,
and had taken my aisle seat on the left side of the central section. I
was extremely nervous and excited by the possibility of seeing the
third of my friend Tom's full-length plays. I had seen the first two,
Candles to the Sun and *Fugitive Kind*, in productions by the Mummers, the little theater group in St. Louis, in 1937. Now this was a
great move forward, for him to have a play sponsored by the Theatre
Guild and directed by the English director Margaret Webster with
the actress Miriam Hopkins in the leading role. I knew that this was
almost a miracle for Tom to have this sort of introduction to the
Broadway scene. It seemed also a miracle that I could be in Boston
for this great occasion. Everything had worked out just the right way
to make it possible. The annual convention of the Modern Language
Association was being held that year at the Ritz-Carlton Hotel in
Boston, and I wanted to be there to meet certain professors from
Princeton and Johns Hopkins University to whom I had introduc-
tions to see if they could not be persuaded to offer me a fellowship
at one or the other place which would make it possible for me to
continue my study of French literature and to avoid being drafted.
I had driven all night from St. Louis with a fellow graduate student
who lived in Providence and had offered to put me up for the night
on the way.

When the play got started, I could well understand why the Theatre Guild had chosen a director who, although she had little experi-

ence with the American South, had worked at length with the poetry of Shakespeare. The poetry in the lines of *Battle of Angels* came
through beautifully delivered by Miriam Hopkins, Doris Dudley,
and the others. But I found it difficult to follow the several threads
of the plot that dealt, as had his previous plays, with the "fugitive
kind." The voluptuous Southern lady, Cassandra Whiteside, like
the classical prophet she represents, addresses Valentine Xavier, the
handsome, gifted poetic drifter who has wandered into the Delta
town: "You and me belong to the fugitive kind. We live in motion.
. . . Nothing but motion, mile after mile, keeping up with the wind."[1]

The playwright had originally called the play *Something Wild in
the Country*, and that something is personified by the handsome, vir-
ile Val Xavier in his snakeskin jacket, who awakens the sexual urge
that religion had held in check in the women of this little Delta community and sets off a symbolic battle between flesh and spirit. The
playwright wants us to feel exactly what it was like in the small town
that he remembers from his boyhood, and so he brings all the senses
into play, every sight and sound is called up: we hear drum beats
and gun shots, follow thunder and lightning, wind and rain, listen to
pinball machines and guitars playing, and catch the constant barking
of "hound-dawgs" tracking fugitives through the woods. All of this
builds up tension like a series of small firecrackers going off one after
the other until they finally reach the big explosion that is the fire that
brings the house down. Tennessee Williams himself describes what
happened in the last scene:

> At the final dress-rehearsal there had not been enough smoke
> to make the fire convincing. Obviously this deficiency had
> been thoroughly impressed upon the gentlemen operating the
> smoke-pots, for on opening night when it came time for the
> store to burn down it was like the burning of Rome. Great
> sulfurous billows rolled chokingly onto the stage and coiled
> over the foot-lights. To an already antagonistic audience this
> was sufficient to excite something in the way of pandemonium.

Outraged squawks, gabbling, spluttering spread through all the front rows of the theatre. Nothing that happened on the stage from then on was of any importance. Indeed the scene was nearly eclipsed by the fumes. Voices were lost in the banging up of seats as the front rows were evacuated.

When the curtain at last came down, as curtains eventually must, I had come to the point where one must laugh or go crazy. I laughed. There was little joy in it, but knowing I had to laugh, I found that I could. Miriam Hopkins accepted the same necessity. I see her coming out to face her audience. The stage is still full of smoke. Before her smiling face she is waving a small white hand, to clear the fumes away. She is coughing a little, apologetically touching her throat and chest. Their backs are turned to her, these elegant first-nighters, as they push up the aisles like heavy, heedless cattle. But she is still gallantly smiling and waving away the smoke with her delicate hand. The curtain bobs foolishly up and down to a patter of hands in the balcony that goes on after the lower floor is emptied.

This is now the historical version of the conclusion of *Battle of Angels*. But I must say that I witnessed little of the pandemonium that the playwright describes. I heard no banging up of seats, no squawks, gabbling, spluttering spreading through the front rows. And since I was at the center of the theater, I saw no elegant first-nighters "pushing up the aisles like heavy, heedless cattle." Rather than pandemonium I found that there was a period of total confusion, as if the audience did not know how to react to what was clearly a terrible blunder on the part of those staging the piece—a sorry spectacle surely—as if it somehow seemed improper to applaud people trapped like the cast in a burning building. So there was a great hush that spread over the audience, a hush broken when Miriam Hopkins stepped forward waving and bowing and her gesture was followed by a strong wave of applause that swept through the house as if to extinguish the blaze.

Of course, I could say nothing of this reaction to Tom. This performance was, and would remain, for him an absolute and total disaster.

When I met Tom after the play, I had never seen him so pale. He looked as if he had been beaten up, both physically and mentally, and had had all the energy pounded out of him. He said that when the smoke had poured into the audience, all he could do was laugh, and that he may well have done at once, but now he no longer had the force even to do that. We met his agent Audrey Wood, who was accompanied by two men, in front of the theater. As we made our way across the Boston Common on that dark cold night, their voices were soothing and full of support, insisting that all was not lost. But the crackling of their footsteps on the icy grass seemed to be saying something else.

When we got to Tom's hotel, he asked that I stay with him for a while, and when we went up to his room, he appeared so suicidal that I dared not leave him alone. He went at once to a suitcase and took out a rather hefty anthology of poetry that looked like a library book, and I thought that it may well have been one that he had borrowed from the Washington University library in St. Louis. It probably was exactly that, as I learned later, like the volume of the *Collected Poems of Hart Crane* that he had purloined there and had retained for the rest of his life. Since no one had checked the book out all the time it had been on the shelf, he felt that the library would have no reason to complain.

He handed the anthology to me and asked me to read to him the poems of John Donne, which I did for the next hour and a half. Why had he chosen Donne rather than Hart Crane or D. H. Lawrence, to whom *Battle of Angels* was dedicated? I wonder if it wasn't returning to Donne as he had after the performance of *Candles to the Sun* for spiritual guidance. At that time Donne's words, "No man is an island, entire of itself; every man is a piece of the continent, a part of the main," might have served as an epigraph for that play. Or he may have been thinking of what William Butler Yeats wrote to Herbert

Grierson about the latter's edition of Donne: "Poems I could not understand or could vaguely understand are now clear and I notice that the more precise and learned the thought the greater the beauty, the passion; the intricacy and subtleties of his imagination are the lengths and depths of the furrow made by his passion. His pedantry and his obscenity—the rock and loam of his Eden—but make us the more certain that one who is but a man like us has seen God." Tom was sorely in need of that kind of vision on that dark night.

Reviewing the opening performance of this play seventy years ago, I turned to what the playwright said about it when it was re-published in 1944:

> I returned post-haste to New York and dived unwittingly into the little maelstrom my play had provoked. I was delighted with the selection of Miss Hopkins for the role of Myra, but I was alarmed that things had gone ahead so rapidly, that casting was already in progress when the script was really only a first draft. I knew that the ending of the play, as it stood, was a melodramatic *tour-de-force*. Conceptually it was fine—the store was set afire and everything went up in the fiery purgation. Yes, very exciting. "A Wagnerian experience," as someone put it in the Guild office. "But how in hell are you going to stage it?" asked Margaret Webster, who had been engaged as director. This question and others were held in abeyance while the production went rocketing ahead.
>
> Toward the end of rehearsals, a series of frenzied conferences were held. Miss Hopkins, who played her part with heartbreaking beauty and something that only a woman of poetic understanding and deep experience could give—whenever the confusion lifted sufficiently to give her a chance to do so—was now becoming definitely frightened. She looked to me for salvation. . . . Oh, if only my head would clear up a little—could only find some lucid interval in this dervish frenzy that

was sweeping us all unprepared into Boston and disaster! But all the conferences only added to my feeling of impotence. ... At last I went to Peggy [Webster] and told her exactly how unable I was to cope with the emergency. "It is too late," I said. "I can't do anything more! If I could get away from all of you for a month—I could return with a new script. But that is not possible, so you will just have to take what there is and do what you can with it."

"Very well," Webster answered, "the store will burn down."

As indeed it did.

He had apparently given some thought many months before in November 1939 to the ending of this play when he was working on it in the attic studio of his family's house in St. Louis. He told his agent Audrey Wood that when he began *Battle of Angels* he had the intention of writing a play that would make a lot of money but he was hoping "that the final result would have some artistic merit as well." He didn't dare leave the manuscript on his desk in the attic for fear that his mother might read it and "launch one of her literary purges."

He told Audrey that the fire motif in the play struck him as being perfectly silly and that the climax of the third act was "sheer melodrama." He considered cutting the act completely, but four days later, he was intending to keep it and call the play *Figures in Flame*.

I could not help thinking how Tom's mentor and mine, Clark Mills, might have reacted if he had attended the Boston rehearsals of *Battle of Angels*. The rehearsal that he did attend in New York had made him quite uneasy since he found that Tom was behaving more like an amused spectator than a serious young playwright watching over his creation. "Sometimes Tom had a naïve quality that shocked me," he said. "In New York, when they were in the midst of what looked like a dress rehearsal—at least they were using props—and Margaret Webster was directing—an actress was carrying around some paintings depicting churches with red steeples. That was all right, but it seemed unnecessary that Tom would be digging me with his elbow, saying, 'Get it? It's symbolism, Freudian symbolism.' This shocked me because it seemed a little naïve that he would have to explain the obvious. And then he would cackle, the way he did."

Tom always referred to *Battle of Angels* as the emotional record of his youth, and he is, of course, at the center of it. The poetic drifter in the snakeskin jacket is given a name, Valentine Xavier, that is derived from that of a distant ancestor of Williams's paternal grandmother's family, whose name was changed to Sevier in England. If, as his brother Dakin claimed, there is a connection to the Spanish-French Xavier lineage, then it is possible that an earlier branch of the family tree was grafted onto the same family that produced the famous Spanish missionary, St. Francis Xavier. Tom always considered *Battle of Angels* one of his best early plays, better even than *The Glass Menagerie.* The manuscript remained on his desk for more than thirty-five years, undergoing revisions and an unsuccessful reincarnation in 1957 as *Orpheus Descending.* In 1960 it was transferred to film as *The Fugitive Kind,* and finally, in 1974, *Battle of Angels* reappeared as a revised and critically successful New York production. A revival in 1988 of *Orpheus Descending* met with extraordinary success in London and New York.

Orpheus Descending contains the following dialogue between Val and Lady (Myra) Torrance, which represents one of the finest poetic depictions of the totally free spirit that he presents in his best work:

VAL: You know they's a kind of bird that don't have legs so it can't light on nothing but has to stay all its life on its wings in the sky? That's true. I seen one once, it had died and fallen to earth and it was light-blue colored and its body was tiny as your little finger, that's the truth, it had a body as tiny as your little finger and so light on the palm of your hand it didn't weigh more than a feather, but its wings spread out this wide but they was transparent, the color of the sky and you could see through them. That's what they call protection coloring. Camouflage, they call it. You can't tell those birds from the sky and that's why the hawks don't catch them, don't see them up there in the high blue sky near the sun!

LADY: How about in gray weather?

VAL: They fly so high in gray weather the Goddam hawks would get dizzy. But those little birds, they don't have no legs at all and they live their whole lives on the wing, and they sleep on the wind, that's how they sleep at night, they just spread their wings and go to sleep on the wind like other birds fold their wings and go to sleep on a tree.... (*Music fades in.*) —They sleep on the wind and ... (*His eyes grow soft and vague and he lifts his guitar and accompanies the very faint music.*) —never light on this earth but one time when they die!

LADY: I'd like to be one of those birds.

VAL: So'd I like to be one of those birds; they's lots of people would like to be one of those birds and never be — corrupted!

LADY: If one of those birds ever dies and falls on the ground and you happen to find it, I wish you would show it to me because I think maybe you just imagine there is a bird of that kind in existence. Because I don't think nothing living has ever been that free, not even nearly. Show me one of the birds and I'll say, Yes, God's made one perfect creature! —I sure would give this mercantile store and every bit of stock in it to be that tiny bird the color of the sky ... for one night to sleep on the wind and—float! —around under th'— stars.²

3

The Glass Menagerie

In April 1946, exactly a year after it had opened to phenomenal success at the Playhouse Theatre in New York, I attended a performance of *The Glass Menagerie* by Tennessee Williams with Laurette Taylor in the role of Amanda Wingfield. Ashton Stevens, reviewing the play for the *Herald-American* when it first opened in Chicago in December 1944, called it "a lovely thing and an original thing. It has the courage of true poetry couched in colloquial prose. It is eerie and earthy in the same breath." He added that in fifty years of first-nighting he had encountered few jolts so "miraculously electrical" as Taylor's portrayal and that he had not been so moved "since Eleanora Duse gave her last performance on this planet." My reaction was equally intense: I sat absolutely transfixed as Laurette Taylor, with every syllable of her insistent, purring Southern speech, every seemingly off-hand but carefully calculated gesture, wove a web of magic. The play was about all those little things in life that get easily broken, and its fragility was encapsulated like ice on winter branches that might snap at any moment.

Years later Arthur Miller said of this play: "It is usually forgotten what a revolution his first great success meant to the New York theater. *The Glass Menagerie* in one stroke lifted lyricism to its highest level in our theater's history, but it broke new ground in another way. What was new in Tennessee Williams was his rhapsodic insistence that form serve his utterance rather than dominating and cramping it. In him the American theater found, perhaps for the first time, an eloquence and an amplitude of feeling. And driving on this newly discovered lyrical line was a kind of emotional heroism; he wanted not to approve or disapprove but to touch the germ of life and celebrate it with verbal beauty."

In bringing verbal beauty to that celebration of life, the poet-playwright had the assistance of a woman he called "the greatest artist of her profession that I have known." The radiance of Laurette Taylor's art had given him, he said, "the same shock of revelation as if the air about us had been momentarily broken through by light from some clear space beyond us."

With the radiance of her art Laurette Taylor had that evening illuminated the character of Amanda Wingfield, and with her, the household that she dominated, her son, the "selfish dreamer," and her daughter, Laura, who was becoming, like a piece of her own glass collection, "too exquisitely fragile to move from the shelf."

These were people I thought I had seen before in St. Louis, a household on the edge of madness, now, by the madness of great lyrical art and the radiance of an inspired performer, brought to life before my eyes.

When Laurette Taylor died, Tom said that it is our immeasurable loss that her performances were not preserved on the modern screen. "The same is true of Duse and Bernhardt, with whom her name belongs. Their glory survives in the testimony and inspiration of those who saw them." But for me it was not just the vision of Laurette Taylor, however interesting, varied, and beautiful it was, it was also the voice, unlike any that I have heard in the theater anywhere, with its light and dark resonance, its comic and tragic notes, that was capable of lifting the listener into the realm of pure poetry.

The only other time in my life that I had responded in such a manner to a great actress was ten years before in February 1936, when with Tom Williams I attended a performance of Alla Nazimova in Ibsen's *Ghosts*, which we witnessed from the third balcony, the "peanut gallery" of the American Theatre in St. Louis. The effect of this performance on the young Tom was such that it was, he said later, "one of the things that made me want to write for the theater." He had found Nazimova's playing "so fabulous, so terrifyingly exciting . . . so moving that I had to go and walk in the lobby during the last act. I'd stand in the door and look in, then I'd rush back to the lobby again." My memory is that rather than rushing back and forth to the lobby, which would have been impossible in any case from the balcony where we were seated, Tom had remained quieter than I had ever seen him, totally dazed, robbed of speech by the hypnotic rhythms of the great Russian actress in the role of Mrs. Alving as she coped with the encroaching madness of her syphilitic son.

The path between *Battle of Angels*, the failure of which I had witnessed in Boston on December 30, 1940, and *The Glass Menagerie* was a path so strewn with obstacles that it seems almost miraculous that they were finally overcome. Williams had arrived in Hollywood in May 1943 at the position his agent Audrey Wood had found for him with the draft of a new play tentatively titled *The Gentleman Caller* and had begun working on it when Pandro Berman at Metro-Goldwyn-Mayer handed him material to rewrite for Lana Turner. He told Audrey Wood that he felt "a little guilty about the time I don't spend on the Turner script and there are days when just looking at it brings on amnesia, anemia, and the St. Vitus dance!" Soon removed from the script, he wrote a story called "Portrait of a Girl in Glass" and the synopsis of a film treatment of what he called *The Gentleman Caller*. (It is fortunate that Metro-Goldwyn-Mayer turned down this first outline of *The Glass Menagerie*, but it is interesting that Williams initially conceived his play in cinematic terms.)

In "Portrait" he wrote, "I don't believe that my sister was actually foolish. I think the petals of her mind had simply closed through fear. I see the faint and sorrowful radiance of the glass, hundreds of little transparent pieces of it in very delicate colors. I hold my breath, for if my sister's face appears among them—the night is hers!" A few months earlier, when his mother informed him of the lobotomy that had been performed on his sister, in his journal he wrote, "Rose. Her head cut open / A knife thrust in her brain."

In setting down *The Gentleman Caller*, he drew on his childhood memories of Clarksdale, Mississippi, where he listened on Sundays to the sermons of his beloved grandfather, Reverend Walter Dakin, and where a friend of the Dakins, Maggie Wingfield, ran two "deluxe boarding houses, and who had a collection of glass animals in her front window, tiny little glass animal figures. When the sun hit them, everyone would remark that they were absolutely gorgeous."

A year later, Audrey Wood offered *The Gentleman Caller* to the successful Broadway producer Eddie Dowling, "not so much for production," she said, "but for an opinion of the playwright's unusual talent." Mrs. Dowling, the comedienne Ray Dooley, read the play and warned her husband that if he did not immediately take an option on it, someone else would. Dowling turned to the critic George Jean Nathan, who had reservations about the play but saw it as a possible vehicle for his friend Julie Haydon, whom he would eventually marry. Nathan's choice for the role of Amanda Wingfield was Laurette Taylor, who had long been in retirement, had taken to drink after the death of her playwright husband and manager, and had made a brief comeback in *Outward Bound*. She had been reading scripts for years but had discovered nothing suitable for herself. But with *The Gentleman Caller* she knew that she had found what she had been waiting for. The play was soon in production, but even after it opened to ecstatic reviews in Chicago, it attracted an audience only after the critics Claudia Cassidy and Ashton Stevens campaigned vigorously to keep it going.

As I walked out of the Playhouse Theatre, Laurette Taylor's magical evocation of the household I had known was broken when I looked up and saw standing on the curb away from the crowd—as if he had himself stepped off the stage or had emerged, a ghost from that earlier era—the author of this memorable play. He smiled and greeted me as he had so many times on his own doorstep. I was so dumbfounded that I seemed to be waking from a dream. I stuttered, "Magnificent! Magnificent!" as I held onto his hand. And then I asked, almost as if it had been something planned when I'd entered the theater, "Will you come have a drink with me at the Algonquin, where I'm staying?"

"Of course," he replied, and once we were seated there with drinks in front of us, he relaxed completely and explained that he had come again to see the production because he had received reports that Julie Haydon, portraying the sister around whom the play revolves, had been over-acting and upsetting the play's delicate balance. He had found this to be true, although, overwhelmed by Laurette Taylor's performance, I hadn't noticed anything of the sort. Julie Haydon, with her emaciated beauty and a facial expression bordering on ecstasy, seemed perfect in the role of Laura for to the character's physical infirmity she brought toward the end of the play a suggestion of oncoming madness. But in Chicago, Laurette Taylor had become annoyed by the adulation that Haydon showed her during curtain calls and had pushed her aside when she first tried to kiss Taylor's hand and then stooped to kiss her skirt. It may have been antics of this sort that Tom had now detected but that had escaped me.

I initially felt somewhat uncomfortable in the presence of the new, successful Tennessee Williams, but he immediately put me at ease and made it clear that for me he was still in every way the young Tom that I had known in St. Louis. He spoke now of that city as if it were shrouded finally in a distant fog, a place to which neither of us would ever really return. He spoke of our years of distress there, but also of our many happy moments. He asked about Clark, and I had to say that during the war years I had lost track of him but I hoped to find him again.

When he asked about my war experience, I told him of the year and a half that I had spent as liaison officer on board the French frigate *La Grandière* in the Atlantic and the Pacific. I told him that I had spent many hours on that ship reciting my poems into the wind. The picture of me rolling with the deck, pouring my soul into the wind while the waves broke over my feet, elicited from him the wild cackle that was so familiar to me. It prompted me to reach into my briefcase and draw forth the copy of the anthology of Oscar Williams, *The War Poets*, which contained a sizeable collection of my poems. He seemed pleased to see that I was still writing poetry. But I felt at the same time embarrassed that I seemed to be calling attention to the fact that his poor eyesight had kept him from serving during the war.

This was one of the many times when he appeared to be annoyed that the powers of the poetry world did not appear to count him as one of them. An awkward moment was followed by much small talk. When he said, "Good-bye," he added, with great warmth, that we should keep in touch; and that, I assured him, I wanted to do and would see that I did.

The next morning when I reviewed in my mind the play that had made such a profound impression on me, I realized that the most important character that is left out of the play, the father who had disappeared, was perhaps more important than any other in the playwright's future development. Tom had said as much in his last speech:

> "I didn't go to the moon [as his mother had wished], I went much further—for time is the largest distance between two places—"
>
> Not long after that I was fired for writing a poem on the lid of a shoebox.
>
> I left St. Louis. I descended the steps of this fire-escape for a last time and followed, from then on, in my father's footsteps, attempting to find in motion what was lost in space.

Lyle Leverich, the playwright's biographer, has concluded:

> Forced by events documented in Tom's home life and in his writings that it was his "hated" father who *most* influenced

him personally ... I can think of nothing that injures more the developing manhood of a young boy, nothing that can be more intensely felt, than the unrequited love of a son for his father. And no mother's or sister's love can replace or compensate for that rupture. It was a loss that Tennessee felt to his dying day, a loss that he projected into the act of creation. The missing ideal of a son in the loving image of his father became instead the identity of the artist in revolt. It was why Tom chose the name Tennessee, deeply impressed as he was with the fighting spirit of this father's Tennessean forebears.

That spirit may be heard distinctly in "Kitchen Door Blues," a comic poem that Tom wrote around the time he was working on *The Glass Menagerie*. It may have been part of a projected Negro libretto or one of the blues songs he promised to write for Libby Holman. When late in his life I asked permission to reprint the poem in an anthology, Tom told me that of all his works it was the one his father liked best. One can understand why; he must have felt that he himself was speaking:

My old lady died of a common cold.
She smoked cigars and was ninety years old.
She was thin as paper with ribs of a kite,
And she flew out the kitchen door one night!

Now I'm no younger'n the old lady was,
When she lost gravitation, and I smoke cigars.
I look sort of peaked, an' I feel kinda pore,
So for God's sake lock that kitchen door!¹

Here the frail little Southern lady immortalized in *The Glass Menagerie* as standing on her front porch ecstatic about jonquils and waiting for gentlemen callers is sent flying out of the back door, the kitchen door. These lines embody perfectly the absent drunken husband's revenge on the domineering little woman who had for so long ruled the roost. In his *Memoirs*, Tom described his mother as marching into his hospital room, "a little Prussian officer in drag" (she was after all the great-granddaughter of German immigrants), and remarked that writers would do well to free themselves from the influence of their powerful mothers. In this poem, one finds the dark underside of *The Glass Menagerie*, and like all the dialogue of the plays, these lines come right off the page. It is the father's voice that one hears, but it is also Tom's voice: I can hear him intoning it and following it up with a loud cackle and resounding laughter. It is a far cry indeed from the clear bell-like tones of the poetry of *The Glass Menagerie*, reminiscent as it is of the lucid lyrics of that other St. Louis poet, Sara Teasdale, whom Tom so admired when I first met him.

Tennessee Williams always felt ambivalent toward *The Glass Menagerie*, once scrawling on a typescript of it "a rather dull little play" too "nice" to represent the drama that he felt he could and should write. Late in his life he said, "It is the saddest play I have ever written. It is full of pain. It is painful for me to see it." Eddie Dowling, who produced it and played in it, was incensed when Audrey Wood gave Irene Mayer Selznick the rights to produce *A Streetcar Named Desire*, and he wrote to a friend that Tennessee Williams "went off with this beautiful sister into Cheap Clap Trap Melodrama aided and abetted by Mr. Kazan, and the strange Audrey Wood. Poor Williams, who would have gone into immortality with Shelley, Keats, Bacon, Goldsmith, and Shaw if he could have kept out of the pig sty." Whether he would have been greater had he eschewed the melodramatic violence of his subsequent work, stemming as it did from his father's rough Tennessean forebears, it is hard to say. But it is clear that he was never again to write a drama couched in such lucid, lyrical prose, reflecting the poetic heritage of Sidney Lanier and so revealing of his youthful and vulnerable self.

4

The Poet, Lyric and Dramatic

Thomas Lanier Williams began to write at the age of twelve in Clarksdale, Mississippi, and the following poem, written two years later in St. Louis, displays his remarkable early grasp of the craft of poetry:

Nature's Thanksgiving

The Bob-White is whirring
And beating, and throbbing;
The wood-brook is singing
And happily sobbing;
The carnival leaves
In resplendent descent,
Fall in a glory o'er merry content.
The wood has all colored,
And flaunting in pride,
Is swaying and laughing
Before they subside
To the sleep—
And the dark—
Of the winter.[1]

The poem appeared in October 1924 in a bi-weekly newspaper *The Junior Life* at Ben Blewett Junior High School, which Tom attended from 1923 to 1926. It is a dramatic, playful appreciation of a woodland landscape before it fades and sinks, along with the brook flowing through it, into the deadly quiet and dark of winter. A quick watercolor done with the lightest of brush strokes, the poem is at the same time a triumph of sound, a little arpeggio dropping abruptly to a serious and somber conclusion.

The opening lines combine at once color and sound. The American quail is called *bob-white* in imitation of the sound it makes. Here the bob-white is *whirring*, making, my *Concise Oxford Dictionary* tells me, "the continuous buzzing or softly clicking sound of birds' wings quickly flapping or cog-wheels in rapid action." The word, of Scandinavian origin, is perhaps related to *whirl*, and that relation prepares the reader for the leaves falling from the trees as from the carnival's circling Ferris wheel.

The poem moves swiftly forward in heavily stressed two-beat lines, their feminine *-ing* endings carried along by a variety of vowels, evoking both the flow of the brook and the fall of the leaves. It is bound together with great subtlety by the three spondees: *Bob-white*, *wood-brook*, and *subside*. *Bob-white* also offers its counterpoint by a stress that falls slightly more heavily on the second word, mimicking the uplifting sound of the quail. *Wood-brook* presents a similar counterpoint by a stress on *brook* for meaning, despite the apparent equivalence of the double *o*'s in both words. A full spondee, *subside*, its two syllables equally heavily stressed, brings down fully and finally the water's flow and the leaves' fall.

The final lines of stress, with their single-beat anapests, end on a two-syllable word that also becomes a spondee:

Tŏ thĕ sléep—
Ănd thĕ dárk—
Ŏf thĕ *wín-tér*.

The somber ending of *sleep, dark,* and *winter* has been anticipated by the *happily sobbing*, tearful joy of the brook, and the wood's *swaying and laughing, flaunting*, showing off its autumnal finery before its proud fall.

If I have spent a long time on what may seem nothing but a trifle, it is because it clearly reveals the early genius of the poet's approach to the theme of the darkening season of autumn as a metaphor for human life. It is a companion piece, a prelude, to the poem that concludes his play *The Night of the Iguana*, "How calmly does the orange branch / Observe the sky begin to blanch." It is worthy of standing beside a similar early piece by William Wordsworth.

In the rectory of the grandfather, the Reverend Dakin Williams, in 1916 in Clarksdale, on the Sunflower River, not far from where De Soto is thought to have first seen the Mississippi River, Rose Williams, then six, and Tom—or "Tommy" as he at the time was to the family—played together happily, catching lightning bugs on summer evenings. The pair—the "couple" as their black nurse Ozzie called them—listened to her singing African spirituals and supplying them with a wealth of black and Indian folklore. Ozzie spoke of "de debil" as a constant inescapable presence. When little Tommy was seen one day digging in the clay, he announced that he was "diggin' to de debbil."

In 1917 when he was ready for school, Tom fell seriously ill—with diphtheria followed by a severe kidney infection. (I have a vivid memory of the horror of diphtheria because my mother contracted it when I was four years old and I recall being ushered through the dark room where she lay and when she finally recovered being confronted by the bucket of her hair that she had lost during her illness.)

Tom was confined to bed for so long that on his seventh birthday in 1918 he could only manage to take a few steps. Tom would never forget that his mother not only saved his life, but, by constantly reading fairy tales, reciting nursery rhymes, and singing Scottish and Irish ballads, also trained his ear and prepared it for the poetry that he would one day himself produce.

"Nature's Thanksgiving" is only the first of many such poetic pieces, and we know precisely in this case where it came from. In his

Notebooks Tom remembers having discussed poetry with his friend Clark Mills in Chicago in 1936. Clark had said, "The only trouble with Romantic poets is that they've been dead and in the dust for about 100 years." "We then talked of Sidney Lanier," Tom said, "[and having] asked if I were related to him, Clark asserted that he had never read anything by the poet but remembered having heard that the 'Marshes of Glynn' was rather good. I know that he was lying about having read nothing by Lanier. Even illiterate people had read 'The Marshes.' It's almost inescapable—and Clark reads *everything* in verse. I admitted that Lanier was a poor poet but expressed admiration for him as a man."

Perhaps at the time Tom did not realize how indebted he was, and would be all his life, to the poet and to the man. In Williams's Thanksgiving ode we hear the echo of one of Lanier's most famous poems, which, along with many other Southern schoolboys, Tom probably knew by heart. Here is the opening stanza of the "Song of the Chattahoochee":

> Out of the hills of Habersham,
> Down the valleys of Hall,
> I hurry amain to reach the plain,
> Run the rapid and leap the fall,
> Split at the rock and together again,
> Accept my bed, or narrow or wide,
> And flee from folly on every side,
> With a lover's pain to attain the plain
> > Far from the hills of Habersham,
> > Far from the valleys of Hall.

John Hollander points out that a favorite poet of Williams, Hart Crane, with his "Repose of Rivers," recast Lanier's stream "as strongly as the earlier poet had recast Tennyson's 'both in "The Brook" and in other lyrics.'"

The grandfather's rectory had, as well as the work of Lanier, the complete works of Shakespeare. Tom read through them all and, in doing so, learned how to make use in his plays, as Shakespeare does in his, of nonsense, which stirs things up and diverts attention momentarily from a plot's tragic direction. In Tom's *Stairs to the Roof*, the lines

Jack be nimble,
Jack be quick,
Jack jump over
Arithmetic!

may seem silly at first and not mean anything at all until one realizes that symbolically they summarize the entire action, and hence are a very appropriate epigraph for the play.

The second of "Two Metaphysical Sonnets," "Le Coeur a ses raisons," written in 1936 and published in the Washington University magazine, *The Eliot*, makes clear Williams's debt to Sidney Lanier:

*Le cœur a ses raisons**

The heart has its own reasons of which the mind
Can never guess the mystical intent.
Why look into the mangled skull to find
Wherefore those atoms toward destruction went
Like chimney swallows whirling toward the sun?
The heart grew tired and so it tired the flesh
Of doing things that were too safely done
And far too often to be done afresh . . .

The mind with all its knowledge cannot know
Wherefore the heart would quit the house of bone
On wings more ghostly than the ghost of snow.
Tossed by the winds, unweaponed, and alone—

---

*"Le cœur a ses raisons que la raison ne connaît point"—Pascal.

The heart has secrets that cannot be known
To his less ancient brother of the bone![2]

The poem is based on the famous quotation from Pascal, which reads, in English: "The heart has its reasons that reason knows nothing of." This quotation occurs several times in the work of Tennessee Williams: It is recited by the heroine at the climax of the story "Two on a Party":

> That is one of those little French sayings that Cora is proud of knowing and often repeats to herself as well as to others.
> Sometimes she will translate it, to those who don't know the French language, as follows:
> The heart knows the scoop when the brain is ignorant of it!

The "scoop" may be a vulgar summary of Lanier's life's work. A victim of the Civil War, Sidney Lanier celebrated the poetic transcendent spirit of his heart while his body was slowly consumed by the tuberculosis that he contracted in the war. For him, as for Tom, the American South represented the human heart, while the triumphant North, with its intellectual and material accomplishments, was the work of the human brain. Lanier stressed the chivalry and honor of the Old South, as Tom does in his story "The Knightly Quest." Lanier was himself a musician, a flautist, and his final work was an essay "The Science of English Verse." For him music was "Love in search of a word." Tom even follows Lanier's footsteps in his dialectic poems of the Southern field hands both black and white.

Tennessee Williams was first and foremost a poet. "I'm a poet," he said proudly in an interview. "And then I put poetry in the drama. I put it in the short stories, and I put it in the plays. It doesn't have to be called a poem, you know." Clark Mills said:

> I think he has more poetry in his plays than in his poetry. And,

in fact, I would say there is a quality that I think is unique to him. It has to do with the *flow* of his language and dialogue. It has some kind of poetic quality to it. I don't know of any other American playwright, living or dead, who has it. This quality was present even in the early days when he would come to my house and write, banging page after page and throwing them on the floor. I'd pick up and read what he'd discarded and there still would be this magic quality to the dialogue—it wasn't the language or the words or the sentences or the way they were put together, it was the "sound" of voice that came through somehow. He seemed to "hear" a voice as much as he heard the words. And I think when you hear the voice like that, you are in the realm of poetry.

This quality derives much from the music of Sidney Lanier, as exemplified in "The Marshes of Glynn," this segment of which Tom used to love to recite:

As the marsh-hen secretly builds on the watery sod,
Behold I will build me a nest on the greatness of God:
I will fly in the greatness of God as the marsh-hen flies
In the freedom that fills all the space 'twixt the marsh and the
skies:
By so many roots as the marsh-grass sends in the sod
I will heartily lay me a-hold on the greatness of God:
Oh, like to the greatness of God is the greatness within
The range of the marshes, the liberal marshes of Glynn.

There were, of course, contemporary poets other than Hart Crane who influenced Thomas Lanier Williams. Among the lyricists were Edna St. Vincent Millay, whose work he praised all his life, and Sara Teasdale, the poet born in St. Louis and long an unhappy resident there, to whom he felt especially close. Almost bare of ornament, her best poems employed the simple direct rhythmic language with which the playwright composed his plays. He followed her life as closely as her work, and when she committed suicide in January 1933, he dedicated this poem to her. It is based on a Teasdale poem in which she says that after she is gone and April "shakes out her rain-drenched hair, though you lean over me broken-hearted, I shall not care."

Under the April Rain
(To Sara Teasdale)

Her heart was a delicate silver lyre
    On which love's fingers played
Songs that were glittering faery fire
    In some dark, mystic glade.

Her song was ever a woman's song,
    Wrung from a woman's breast,
That argued never a right nor wrong,
    But sung our hearts to rest.

Her ashes we scattered upon the sea,
    As song is spilt on air;
But under the April rain she is free,
    She is silent, and does not care![3]

Tom wrote many poems during the 1930s and 1940s that showed the direct influence of Sara Teasdale. In none of these is his close reading of her work more apparent than in "Dear Silent Ghost," a poem that he perhaps began much earlier but apparently completed shortly after the death of his grandmother ("Grand," as he called her) in 1944. The image of the April air he had used in his play *Candles to the Sun* in 1937, and it was still fresh with him years later:

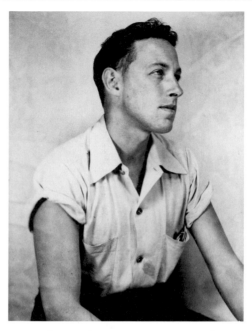

Tennessee Williams as he was in 1935 when WJS first met him at Washington University in St. Louis.

Painting of Rose Williams by Florence Ver Steeg, St. Louis, 1937.

Clark Mills McBurney, Washington University, St. Louis, 1935.

William Jay Smith, c. 1937, at Washington University, St. Louis.

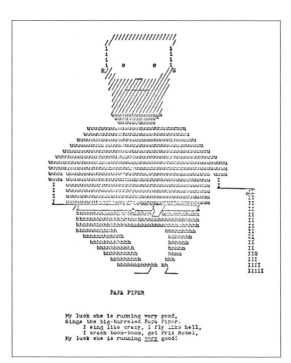

PAPA PIPER

My luck she is running very good,
Sings the big-barreled Papa Piper.
    I sing like crazy, I fly like hell,
    I crash boom-boom, get Prix Nobel,
My luck she is running *very* good!

William Jay Smith's typewriter portrait of Ernest Hemingway, from *Literary Birds* (1957). Courtesy of the Ruth and Marvin Sackner Archive of Concrete and Visual Poetry.

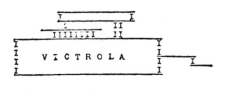

```
        I                I
        I          II
        IIIIIIII   II
  I ┌─────────────────┐ I
  I │                 │ I
  I │  V I C T R O L A │ I          I
  I │                 │ I ─────── I ───────
  I └─────────────────┘ I
  I                     I


          GOLDEN-THROATED EDNA

               (Recording)


O world, I cannot hold thee close enough!
Enough! . . .Enough! . . .Enough! . . .Enough! . . .Enough!
```

William Jay Smith's typewriter portrait of Edna St. Vincent Millay, from *Literary Birds* (1957). Courtesy of the Ruth and Marvin Sackner Archive of Concrete and Visual Poetry.

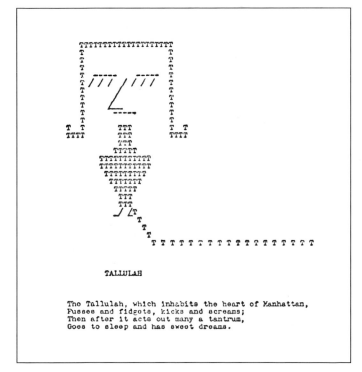

William Jay Smith's typewriter portrait of Tallulah Bankhead, from *Literary Birds* (1957). Courtesy of the Ruth and Marvin Sackner Archive of Concrete and Visual Poetry.

Scene from the Washington University performance of Molière's
Les Fourberies de Scapin, April 1937, in which Smith (*center*) played Scapin
and Williams (*fourth from right*) played the old father.

William Jay Smith in St. Louis, June 1942.
Having just been named an ensign in the U.S. Naval Reserve after
three months of training in Chicago, he was preparing to leave for
his first assignment at Pearl Harbor, Hawaii.

Frank Merlo, as he was in 1949, when he drove
with Tennessee Williams from Rome to Florence
to visit WJS and wife, Barbara Howes.

Frank Merlo and Tennessee Williams, Key West, 1955, in the Buick
in which they drove from Rome to Florence in 1949.

Still from Jean-Claude van Itallie's play *America Hurrah*, 1966.

Tennessee Williams at Lynchburg College, Virginia, 1979.

Tennessee Williams as he was in 1977, when he returned for the first time to Washington University in St. Louis.

Tennessee Williams's tombstone, Calvary Cemetery, St. Louis.

Burial at sea of a French sailor, off the coast of Panama, on board the French frigate *La Grandière*, on which WJS served as American liaison officer, June 1945.

Dakin Williams, Tennessee's brother, and WJS at the Tennessee Williams Festival, New Orleans, March 2004.

Rose Williams's gravestone, next to her brother's, Calvary Cemetery, St. Louis.

Dear Silent Ghost

I see you scraping carrots by the stove
Or spicing meats with cinnamon and clove. . . .

Through memory your patient hands are spun
Lifting white curtains to the morning sun

Or beckoning at twilight from the stair. . . .
I feel your rain-washed, lemon-scented hair

Cool on my cheeks, heated and flushed from play
In April woods, some far, nostalgic day. . . .

But where, Dear Silent Ghost, are put away
The wise and lovely things you used to say?

Behind the stove or underneath the stair. . .
In lemon scent or rain-washed April air?[4]

The poet Vachel Lindsay also interested Tom. For years Lindsay
had been a great admirer of Teasdale and, after corresponding with
her for years, had failed to convince her to marry him and to follow
him to his home in Springfield, Illinois. She married instead Ernst
Filsinger, a wealthy St. Louis shoe manufacturer. Unfortunately,
that marriage ended in divorce. In New York, where she was in 1931,
Sara Teasdale learned that when Lindsay's subsequent marriage was
also about to end in divorce, he had taken his life by drinking Lysol,
she wrote an elegy for him in which she quotes from "The Chinese
Nightingale," which he had dedicated to her in 1914 and which he
had called "The Best Song of My Days." Fourteen months later Sara
Teasdale was discovered dead in her bath, having taken an overdose
of sleeping pills.

At Washington University Tom, Clark, and I were friends of Catherine and Mary Lois, the nieces of Ernst Filsinger. If Tom knew of their connection to the wealthy manufacturer, he never mentioned it to us. The lives of these two poets represented for Thomas Lanier Williams the destiny of all American artists. He wrote at length to his agent Audrey Wood about a play he was planning based on Lindsay's life. In his application for a Rockefeller Fellowship it was one of the plays in progress that he mentioned. Williams found particularly appealing the figure of Lindsay, the wandering bard going from door to door to peddle his poems that he offered in a pamphlet titled *Rhymes to be Traded for Bread*. When these poems were published in Lindsay's first trade volume, *General William Booth Enters into Heaven and Other Poems* (1913), they inspired the young St. Louis poet. If you wonder if any modern poet before Williams had called attention to the outcasts of society, the crazy, the queer, the unclean, the drugged, the untouchable like the lepers, you will find them all portrayed in Lindsay's poem, as he put it, "every soul resident—For the earth's circus tent." The outcasts resoundingly presented by Lindsay are echoed in many poems of Tennessee Williams, of which this one written in 1952 while he was staying with Maria Britneva is a moving example:

A Big Storm

A big storm blew
the wires down
so I ran screaming
through the town.

Unclean, unclean!
and rang my bell
that lepers wear
to say, Not well!

And when my tongue
is blown away,
if there is more
I want to say,

I have an eyeball
that can stare
and a tuft of
sun-bleached hair

With which I'll make
a flag to wave
upon a staff of
splintered bone.

I'll wave it in
a field alone
as if to signal
all unknown

That people laugh at,
at whom they stare,
all shouting scarecrows,
skinny, bare

As buildings blasted,
crying dumb,
Cassandra's played
by Thomas Thumb. . . .[5]

Tennessee Williams was a lyric poet. Lyric poetry, because its
language is simple and direct, does not date. The poems he wrote,
like those of Herrick or Shakespeare, sound as if they were written

yesterday or as they will sound as if written a hundred years from now. The same is true of those of Williams. In this one written in November of 1937 he foresaw his entire life, which he presented as a "boundless continent" that he contemplated in "the early morning of the mind." The images of the eagles at dawn, the hissing serpent, and the moths fluttering the blinds occur in several later poems. There are many other short lyrics that he inserted in his plays and many that he simply discarded. It would be well if one day the best of these might be brought together in a single volume as the straightforward direct songs that they are, without academic commentary but solely for the reader's enjoyment as one of the lasting contributions of the poet.

Odyssey

It seemed infinity to him
With eagles crying in the dawn:
Importunately then he dreamed
Of lands forever leading on!

A boundless continent was this,
The early morning of the mind—
But evening heard a serpent hiss
Or moth wings fluttering the blind,

And presently the pilgrim turned
Exhausted toward the nearest gate
And as a final lesson learned
That even Death could make him wait![6]

Tennessee Williams knew that he was, before all else, a poet, and when he was not recognized and accepted as one, he was deeply hurt. When his first book of poems, *In the Winter of Cities*, appeared in 1956, it was dismissed by several well-known poet-critics, and from then on, he had little good to say of most published poets. Even one like me whom he knew and approved of he could not refrain from calling "a poet of prominence," which meant actually that I was just one of the sad lot that had rejected him. At the end of his life when at numerous readings of his poetry he received standing ovations, he could not believe that they really meant full appreciation and acceptance.

No one has spoken more succinctly and directly of the poetic quality of the work of Tennessee Williams than John Simon did on the playwright's death, and it is unusual to have this commentary from one of the critics who had had little good to say of many of the plays when they first appeared:

> Most typical of the poet [. . .] is the headily lyrical experience of the moment, the enshrinement of the instant as a symbol of eternity, or of such part of it as the mortal being can encompass. When you think of it, *The Glass Menagerie*—all of it—is subsumed by, or consumed in, the moment when the Gentleman Caller breaks the horn off Laura's precious glass unicorn, and the deeply wounded girl merely says, "Now he will feel more at home with the other horses, the ones that don't have horns. . . ." How richly that incident and line irradiate the entire play! Here is the shattering of Amanda's foolish illusions about her daughter's being special. Here is the end of hope that Jim, or anyone, will ever marry Laura. Here is the tragedy of life, which prevents us from surviving in our peculiar uniqueness; here, too, the comedy of life, which cuts us down to indistinguishability from the herd. And here is the resignation that tames heartbreak with the caress of a metaphor. A play that thinks in images is a truly poetic play, and no other American dramatist, not even O'Neill, quite managed that.

And as one who has admired his work from the beginning, I can only agree with Simon when he says in conclusion:

I am deeply saddened, though not entirely surprised, that his end should have been so bizarre and, no doubt, painful and frightening. But, at any rate, like everything else about him, it was out of the ordinary. And from now on, the immortal part of his work will not merely continue; it will also, as we explore it further, grow.

5

A Streetcar Named Desire

In the spring of 1947, a year after I had attended the performance of *The Glass Menagerie* with Tennessee Williams, I was back in New York. I was teaching courses in French and English at Columbia University, where I had enrolled as a graduate student in English with a plan for taking a PhD in English and comparative literature. Tallulah Bankhead had made such an impression on me when I had gone with Tom to see her in *The Little Foxes* in St. Louis in 1940 that I was thrilled to read about her latest undertaking. She was appearing in *The Eagle Has Two Heads*, a play written by Jean Cocteau, which had been performed with great success in Paris in 1946, with Edwige Feuillère as the Queen and Jean Marais as Stanislas, the anarchist poet. An English adaptation done by Ronald Duncan opened in September in London with Eileen Herlie as the Queen and James Donald as Stanislas. The anthem for this production was written by Benjamin Britten, and the play was transferred into the Haymarket Theater in February 1947 and subsequently to the Globe Theater, where it ran with success until July 1947. Tallulah's version was on its way to Wilmington, Delaware, to Washington, D.C., and to Boston in December 1946.

Jean Cocteau had apparently been inspired by the stories of Ludwig II of Bavaria, who drowned in Lake Stamberg under unexplained circumstances, and the Empress Elizabeth of Austria, who was stabbed in the back while walking in Geneva. In focusing on the themes of love and death, he had wanted to create characters who would demand the grand style of acting that was declining in the French theater, as it was in the English and American theaters. He certainly found the perfect performer in Edwige Feuillère, whom Tennessee Williams considered one of the three greatest actresses in his plays, the other two being Laurette Taylor and Anna Magnani.

Tallulah Bankhead was one of the few American women who could perform in the grand manner. Here, as the Queen, she holds forth nonstop in a monologue of approximately twenty minutes at the top of the royal stairway. Then the moment the assassin's bullet reaches her back, she lurches toward the window where she makes a final appearance to her public while the national anthem is played. Then, wrapping herself in the drapery that she pulls from the windows, she tumbles headfirst down the stairs.

In Wilmington, Delaware, where the play opened, Marlon Brando, who had been hired to play the part of Stanislas, behaved very strangely. When the company manager invited him to share a cab to go to the Hotel DuPont, Brando declined. He needed a cab of his own so that he could travel around town for the next hour practicing his African drums. He apparently hated the play and hated his part in it and did everything he could think of to call attention to himself and away from Tallulah. When it came time for him to die and follow the Queen tumbling down the stairs, he spent endless time wobbling around the set. One Boston critic said that he was like a car caught in midtown Manhattan traffic looking for a parking place. Before his fall, he turned his back on the audience, opened his fly and urinated on the scenery. Tallulah had him immediately replaced by the German actor Helmuth Dantine.

At the end of August 1947, no actor had been found for the role of Stanley Kowalski in *A Streetcar Named Desire*, which was ready for production. Bill Liebling suggested the twenty-three-year-old Marlon Brando, a former New School student in Erwin Piscator's Drama Workshop. Brando had been in just four Broadway productions, which Liebling very much approved of: first, as the son in *I Remember Mama*; second, in Maxwell Anderson's *Truckline Café*, directed by Harold Clurman and coproduced by Clurman and Elia Kazan, in 1946; third, in Ben Hecht's salute to Israel, *A Flag Is Born*, with Paul Muni, also in 1946; and, finally, in a revival of Shaw's *Candida*. His fifth performance in *The Eagle Has Two Heads* was forgotten or ignored, and Brando was invited to come to Provincetown to read for the part.

"I never saw such raw talent in an individual," Williams recalled. "Brando was a gentle, lovely guy, a man of extraordinary beauty when I first met him. He was very natural and helpful. He repaired the plumbing that had gone on the whack, and he repaired the lights that had gone off. And then he just sat calmly down and began to read [the role of Stanley in *A Streetcar Named Desire*]."

Arthur Miller, who saw the play on its tryout in New Haven before it went to New York, said, "The play, more than any of Williams's works before or afterward, approached tragedy, and its dark ending is unmitigated. Along with Williams, the other great revelation of the performance was of course Brando, a tiger on the loose, a sexual terrorist. Nobody had seen anything like him before because that kind of freedom on the stage had not existed before. He roared out Williams's celebratory terror of sex, its awful truthfulness and its inexorable judgments, and did so with an authority that swept everything before it."[1]

Shortly after the successful opening of *The Glass Menagerie* in Chicago, Tennessee Williams began to work on a new play, which he called tentatively *The Moth*, with Tallulah Bankhead again in mind as its doomed heroine Blanche. He stopped working on it after about a week. Soon after *The Glass Menagerie* opened successfully in New York, he left for a visit to the popular fishing resort of Lake Chapala, about thirty miles southeast of Guadalajara, in Mexico. There he started work on the new play again and then called it *Blanche's Chair in the Moon*. The main controlling image in his mind was that of a woman sitting with folded hands near a window while moonlight streams in around her and she awaits in vain the arrival of her boyfriend. It may now seem a very long way from that quiet moonlit beauty to the passion of *Streetcar*, but a newfound sexual violence made the movement possible.[2]

When, in his mind, he moved from the window from which his troubled sister Rose gazed out, waiting for a gentleman caller, to the window opening onto one of those little offices where his father, Cornelius, and his buddies started to play poker as they did night after night after having worked there during the entire day, everything took on new life. According to Randy Echols, one of the stage hands in the Broadway production, "Tennessee wanted to learn how to play poker. He invited some of the crew from the play to his hotel room, provided cards and chips and liquor and food, and then went from player to player taking notes. We found out later what he was doing and why he needed to learn."[3] During the summer the play's name changed to *Poker Night*, and its setting is described in scene 3, under that heading.

The Poker Night

There is a picture of Van Gogh's of a billiard-parlor at night. The kitchen now suggests that sort of lurid nocturnal brilliance, the raw colors of childhood's spectrum. Over the yellow linoleum of the kitchen table hangs an electric bulb with a vivid green glass shade. The poker players—Stanley, Steve, Mitch and Pablo—wear colored shirts, solid blues, a purple, a red-and-white check, a light green, and they are men at the peak of their physical manhood, as coarse and direct and powerful as the primary colors. There are vivid slices of watermelon on the table, whiskey bottles and glasses. The bedroom is relatively dim with only the light that spills between the portières and through the wide window on the street. For a moment, there is absorbed silence as a hand is dealt.

It is well to remember that Tennessee Williams often begins to work on fragments of plays which are brought into place and into focus many months later. For his assignments for a class of Edward Charles Mabie, head of the Theater Department at the University of Iowa in 1938, he had already contemplated writing a play on Vincent Van Gogh, "for which I have chosen the title 'The Holy Family' suggested by an anecdote from his life. He took a prostitute to live with him who soon gave birth to an illeg. [*sic*] child by another man. V. G.'s friend, Gauguin, tried to persuade him to leave the woman but V. G. remained devoted to her. In disgust, as he left, the friend exclaimed, 'Ah! The Holy Family—maniac, prostitute, and bastard!' Does that sound too profane? I think the real story of the relationship is rather beautiful and would make good dramatic material." One can see how thought of it provides the primary colors that are brought to bear right here.

Poker, the great American card game, apparently derives its name from the German *pochen*, meaning to beat or beat up or pulverize. A prime example of this would be the game in which Cornelius had one of his ears chewed off and had to be rushed to the hospital to have it sewn back on.

The scene of "Poker Night" was brilliantly painted by the Missouri painter Thomas Hart Benton in 1948, after the play had opened on Broadway. The painting, which now hangs in the Whitney Museum, is an authentic piece of Americana, given as a Christmas present to Irene Selznick, the producer of *Streetcar*, by her estranged husband, David Selznick. The Signet paperback edition, to publicize the film version of *A Streetcar Named Desire* (1951), used a color reproduction of the painting portraying the Broadway cast that had caused some upset, in particular from Jessica Tandy, who found the painting to be an inaccurate and over-sexualized interpretation of Blanche. I think that she should not have been concerned in this way. The scene does indeed portray Blanche, as she certainly was, as an extraordinary beautiful woman, but one hand lifts the mirror toward her face to gaze upon her beauty while her other hand holds her head high as if she were truly in touch with the poetry, art, and music that accompany her when she departs for the Elysian Fields or the asylum. The triangle of her arms is echoed by that below of Brando, who waits with all the animal baseness which will bring her down to the death that she knows awaits her.

Arthur Miller is correct in saying, "On first hearing *Streetcar*—and one truly heard every word of it in that first production, unlike some others that have followed over the years—the impression was not that of one-liners or 'poetry' but of language flowing from the soul. A Writer's soul, a single voice was almost miraculously enveloping the stage." Tennessee said later, "I draw all my characters from myself, I can't draw a character unless I know it within myself." And as Elia Kazan well understood, "Blanche DuBois the woman, *is* Williams. Blanche comes into a house where someone is going to murder her. The interesting part of it is that Blanche DuBois is *attracted* to the person who is going to murder her. I saw Blanche as Williams, an ambivalent figure who is attracted to the harshness and vulgarity around him at the same time that he fears it, because it threatens his life."[4]

6

Williams and Frank Merlo

I have often regretted that I did not write more frequently to Tennessee Williams. When I did, he responded immediately with the warmth and wit to which I was accustomed. This last letter to me I have set down just as it was when it arrived; it was addressed from the Shakespeare Motor Inn in Stratford, Connecticut, where *Cat on a Hot Tin Roof* was being revived before being transferred to the ANTA Theatre in New York.

July 18, 1974 [written by hand across right side of page]
Dear Bill:
AS USUAL I'VE LOST SOMETHING, THIS TIME
MY READING GLASSES, SO THAT I HAVE
TO WRITE IN CAPS TO MAKE OUT WHAT
I'M WRITING. I'D ONLY READ ONE OF THE
ESSAYS BEFORE, THE ONE ABOUT LOUISE
BOGAN, AND AM DELIGHTED TO HAVE A
CHANCE TO ENJOY THEM ALL. I AM SO AC-
CUSTOMED, BILL, TO MISQUOTATIONS, NOT
TO MENTION THE ENDLESS CALUMNIES,
THAT THE LINES YOU HAVE RESURRECTED
FROM MY FUNNIEST PIECE OF VERSE SEEM
ALMOST FAITHFUL TO THE TEXT, AL-
THOUGH THEY DON'T QUITE SCAN. THEY
WENT LIKE THIS. "YET, DEATH, I'LL PARDON
ALL YOU TOOK AWAY / WHILE STILL YOU

SPARE ME GLORIOUS MILLAY!"
YOUR NEW POSITION AT COLUMBIA SOUNDS
GREAT AND I HOPE IT WILL MAKE IT POS-
SIBLE FOR US TO MEET AGAIN AFTER THIS
LONG INTERVAL. YOU MENTION SONJA IN
YOUR LETTER. WHEN I SAW YOU IN FLOR-
ENCE, YOU WERE MARRIED TO A GIRL
NAMED BARBARA, LOVELY AND A POET. I
HOPE NOTHING SAID [sic] IS INVOLVED. DO
YOU EVER HEAR ANYTHING ABOUT CLARK?
YOU AND HE MADE ST. LOUIS ENDURABLE TO
ME IN THOSE DAYS, AND THAT TOOK A LOT
OF DOING. YOU MAY REMEMBER I DIDN'T
EVEN HAVE A HOUSE KEY. AND THE STORIES
OF GORDON SAGER AND DR. FRANK WEB-
STER WERE THE SCANDAL OF OUR LIVES.
WHEN IN NEW YORK I STAY AT THE HOTEL
ELYSEE, 60 E. 54TH STREET, A SHRINE TO
MANY OLD ACTRESSES SUCH AS ETHEL BAR-
RYMORE, TALLULAH, DOROTHY GISH. I'M
NOT SURE THAT GLORIOUS MILLAY EBER [sic]
HUNG HER HARP THERE.
    GOOD LUCK AND LOVE,
        Tom

I had sent Tom a copy of my book *The Streaks of the Tulip: Se-*
lected Criticism that had appeared in 1972. The volume had included
an essay on the work of Louise Bogan. I had remembered that in St.
Louis Tom and I had both admired her poems in the *New Yorker*,
where she regularly reviewed poetry. I had since then become a
friend of hers and we had edited together an anthology of poetry for
children, *The Golden Journey*. In a footnote to my essay I had quoted
from memory a poem about women poets that Tom had written

before we met. I had apologized for having misquoted him. Here in his response he correctly quotes the closing couplet to his sonnet, which he later published in its entirety in his *Memoirs*, with these words introducing it:

> During the weekdays [from 1931 to 1934 when he was employed, at his father's insistence, at the Continental Shoemakers] I would work on verse: quite undistinguished, I fear, and upon one occasion, I knocked out what is probably the most awful sonnet ever composed. It strikes me, now, as comical enough to be quoted in full:

> I see them lying sheeted in their graves,
> All of the women poets of this land,
> Each in her inscrutable small cave,
> Song reft from lip and pen purloined from hand.
> And no more vocal, now, than any stone,
> Less aureate, in fact, now, than winter weed,
> This thing of withered flesh and bleached bone
> That patterned once beauty's immortal creed.

> Rudely death seized and broke proud Sappho's lyre,
> Barrett and Wylie went their songless way,
> He does not care what hecatomb of fire
> Is spilt when, shattering the urn of clay.
> Yet, Death, I'll pardon all you took away
> While still you spare me glorious Millay.

Although here Tom makes fun of Millay, I recall the afternoon in St. Louis when Clark, he, and I had read with great admiration the poems of Millay that had just appeared in *Harper's* magazine.

He speaks in his letter of the time in 1949 when, at my suggestion, he drove up from Rome with Frank Merlo to visit Barbara Howes, my first wife, and me, in Florence. He had announced the visit in a letter dated March 5, 1949, from Rome to his friend, the actress Maria Britneva (later St. Just):

> Tomorrow we are leaving for Florence to visit an old school-
> mate of mine, Bill Smith, who is a poet and is married to a
> young lady poet, and they both live in a villa on a hill, I suppose
> both of them writing mad sonnets about spring in Tuscany, but
> the wife is now pregnant so evidently the relationship is not
> strictly one of iambics. Her name is Barbara. Do you suppose I
> will get along with her at all?[1]

He need not have worried about that. She made a great hit with him both as a person and as a poet. When she sent him her next book, he wrote back to tell her that he thought that she was "about the best" of the new American poets.

I shall never forget the sight of Tom arriving in his huge open roadster—a new Buick, of which he was justly proud—with Frank Merlo at the wheel and Tom in dark glasses staring straight ahead, making their way through the narrow streets. The crowd that gathered gazed open-mouthed with delight and amazement at this gorgeous vehicle, the like of which no one had ever seen before. They had driven in the Buick not long before coming to Florence, to Sicily to meet Frank's parents. In another letter to Maria Tom had described his time there: "Don't see or talk to anybody. Work in the morning, enjoy the sun in the afternoons, cruising dreamily about in the Buick, which hangs together after all its crossings so well that it is continually greeted by cries of Que [sic] Bella Machina!"[2] The same cries greeted it in Florence. The city had suffered somewhat during the war, but had been saved by the German general who had failed to carry out Hitler's order to blow up the Ponte Vecchio. The ends of the bridge were, however, still there, in ruins, and a wooden ramp had replaced the beautiful Santa Trinità bridge that was no more.

The question about Clark was one that Tom put to me whenever we met, and there was little that I could tell him but that Clark had retired from teaching and from administration—from Hunter College and Farleigh Dickinson—and had married an attractive Filipina after two divorces and spoke always warmly of his days working with Tom in St. Louis.

The stories of Gordon Sager and Dr. Frank Webster that were, Tom wrote, "the scandal of our lives," seemed far less scandalous in retrospect. Gordon Sager was one of our associates who had contributed poems to the campus magazine *The Eliot*. Having returned from a first visit to New York, he was happy and proud to announce to one and all that he was a homosexual. Dr. Frank Webster taught a night class in the short story that Tom attended when he first enrolled at the university. The widely circulated rumor that Webster was also homosexual appeared to be based on the fact that he was popular, having been made a dean of students, that he was particularly fond of poetry, and that he had occasionally invited handsome young men to his apartment. Homosexuality, in any case, was frowned upon by the members of Clark's group. Clark clearly had great success with women, and we were eager to follow his example and not be one of those whom he dismissed as being simply "neurotic."

When Tom returned to St. Louis for Christmas after his first semester in Iowa, he took me up to the study that had been arranged for him in the attic of the house at 53 Arundel Place in Clayton, which his father had purchased. He spoke with great excitement about the love affair that he was having with an Iowa student, Elizabeth Mary "Bette" Reitz. This affair was his first real sexual experience and he was thrilled by it. Things changed very quickly when he returned to Iowa. In his *Notebooks* he wrote: "After she had irrevocably dismissed me in favor of the new stud, I tried to date other girls. Somehow I didn't manage." During an interval between October 1937 and April 1938, Tom added in his *Notebooks* this entry: "Sometime during this interval the course of my life subtly and definitely changed. I began to integrate more firmly—to grow more independent, detached, sophisticated, a deep physical love affair with a girl and freedom from home were important factors." Tom returned to the subject again in 1979 in his *Notebooks* and it is worth quoting the entire passage:

> I could have been passably "normal"—(I loved Hazel Kramer from the age of eleven till she married a likeable Irishman at the University of Wisconsin.) Now both of them are dead. At the University of Iowa I had my single consummated love-affair with a girl and while that went on, for several months, I lost all interest in boys, with the probable exception of Lemuel Ayres. But there's no doubt that homosexuality of a sensual sort is my nature luckily I would say—for otherwise I'd have an alimony problem as big as Norman Mailer's. . . . Most deeply (after Hazel) were two extraordinary women Marion Black and Maria Britneva, now known as the Lady St. Just. It is sadly true that the latter of these two ladies appears to me, now, to have settled for things unacceptable unimpressive to me: grandeur title and wealth by marriage. But dear Marion is dead. Maria is intensely and fiercely alive. I am in transit, my work prematurely finished.

Maria St. Just was still very much alive when Tom died, and she had been named in his will as one of the trustees of his estate. As such, she was extremely difficult to deal with and during her lifetime prevented the publication of *Tom: The Unknown Tennessee Williams*, the authorized biography of Williams by Lyle Leverich. It was in this book that Leverich discusses in detail a knock-down drag-out fight that Tom had with a classmate who had taken possession of "Bette" while he was away. Apparently Tom had not given her up easily.

I never discussed homosexuality with Tom, but it was clear to him that I very much approved of his relationship with Frank Merlo. What I did not tell him was that Clark also learned early on of Tom's attraction to men. On his way to Cornell in December 1940 he stopped off in New York to visit Tom, who was in the midst of rehearsals for the *Battle of Angels* that was to open shortly in Boston. In the apartment where he was awaiting Tom, Clark opened a note on the piano that he thought was a message for him. It was an impassioned love letter addressed to another man and signed "10" (for Tennessee). Clark told me later, as far as he was concerned, Tom's sexual preference would not have had any affect on their friendship. "Obviously, Tom was constrained," he said, "and it was unfortunate that something that need not come between us ultimately did."

But to return to Florence and the visit of Tom and Frank Merlo in March 1949: Truman Capote and his friend Jack Dunphy were also in Florence at the time, and we invited them to join Tom and Frank for dinner in the villa we had rented in the village of Pian' dei Giullari, up above the city, where the Medici once housed the court jesters. The first problem was how to get them there in their spectacular Buick through the narrow, walled streets. We arranged to have them drive in and park at our neighbors' place, fittingly called in this instance "the Villa Barbara." It was occupied by Elizabeth Marangoni, the daughter-in-law by marriage of the distinguished Italian poet Eugenio Montale, who later received the Nobel Prize.

Looking back, I can see that it was an extraordinary coincidence to have these four people together and all on such good terms. Jack Dunphy was the partner of Truman Capote for thirty years and on Truman's death in 1984 was the chief beneficiary of his estate. When Frank Merlo, who had been Tom's partner for fourteen years, died, Tom wrote in his *Memoirs*: "As long as Frank was well, I was happy. He had a gift for creating a life and when he ceased to be alive, I couldn't create a life for myself. So I went into a seven-year depression." Maureen Stapleton said: "Frank Merlo was a man everyone adored, it's really as simple as that. . . . I became a friend of Tom by being a friend of Frankie. He was the liaison officer between Tom and the rest of the world. He was at home with everyone, easy to be with, uncomplicated and understanding. And he loved and protected Tenn and did everything for him." Christopher Isherwood expressed exactly what Barbara and I felt that night: "Everyone who met Frank Merlo found him a marvelous man. He was a support to Tennessee; he made everything work for him. He ran the house; he looked after him in a way that was uncanny. He was no goody-goody. He was just plain good. And he wasn't just some kind of faithful servitor. He was a lovable man with a strong will. We have a saying in Britain —'he kept his wig on' —that is, he was a man who kept cool, even when he and Tennessee were exposed to the most appalling pressures of social and professional life."

In a letter shortly before coming to Florence, Tom had written to Maria Britneva: "I am glad that we have made it up, for I enjoyed your letters enormously, especially the last one about your strange life in New York and the crack about Truman [Capote]'s voice being so high that only a dog could hear it. Even people who don't know Truman and there are a few who don't, get a terrific laugh out of that one. I guess it is so graphic it presents a complete image, all except the yards of Bronzini neckwear. I once told him he was going to die like Isadora Duncan who also wore one of those things and it got caught in the wheel of a car in which she was making a very grand departure and it promptly broke her neck. Ha ha." Truman spoke fondly of Tom on many occasions, but toward the end of his life in his unfinished novel, *Answered Prayers*, he painted a horrible repulsive picture of him and of the messy life that he was leading. On this evening all four of the group seemed to see each other in the brightest light.

After dinner we retired to our brilliant, gilded living room, where we gathered around the fire, whose golden flames made the walls all the brighter. Barbara and I answered the invitation of our guests to read aloud some of our new work. Barbara read a number of poems from her recent book, *The Undersea Farmer*, and I read a selection of my translations of the Pierrot poems of Jules Laforgue, which had influenced T. S. Eliot. I told the group that Tom's friend and publisher, James Laughlin of New Directions, had expressed an interest in publishing these translations. Reading them reminded me, as it surely did Tom, of the staged reading at Washington University of Eliot's *Murder in the Cathedral*, in which we participated in 1936, shortly after it appeared, and of our discussion with Clark Mills of "The Love Song of J. Alfred Prufrock." Eliot had written at Harvard that poetic presentation of a loneliness and frustration similar to Tom's. Born and reared in St. Louis, Eliot owed a great deal to that city and to the river beside it. What I did not know then was the name he had given the speaker of this monologue was that of a prominent St. Louisan. I discovered recently that on the list of supporting playgoers in the program at the American Theater, where in 1940 Tom and I saw Tallulah Bankhead in *The Little Foxes*, were the names of Mr. and Mrs. Henry Prufrock. Those names would no doubt have also been in the program of 1936 when we saw Alla Nazimova there in Ibsen's *Ghosts*.

Tom asked the next morning about the interesting women in Florence, and I told him about Delphine Jenkins, the most popular hostess, who was the stepmother of the resident composer Newell Jenkins. As a nurse, she had cared for his father and as a result had inherited a goodly portion of the Colgate Toothpaste fortune, which she was happily spending in Florence. When asked about her, I told Tom that she was "desperately trying to be like Billie Burke." Indeed many of her antics became the basis of the play and the movie of "Auntie Mame." She immediately appealed to Tom, and she invited us all to an evening of Chinese food, which we consumed seated in a circle on the floor of her villa.

A little footnote to our dinner party. Our cook Maria came to us sad-faced the following morning. She was sorry, she said, to have learned of the death of our president. What on earth did she mean, we asked; we had heard no such news. In explanation she extended to us a copy of the dust jacket of Truman's recent book that she found in the wastebasket. "*Peccato*," she said. "*Truman Kaput!*"

Truman Capote and Tennessee Williams were not the first literary visitors to Il Fortino. The previous autumn, Sinclair Lewis had come to lunch with an orange-gray-haired lady, Mrs. Powers, his traveling companion. She was the mother of Marcella Powers, twenty-seven years younger than he, whom he had for years wanted to marry. Mark Schorer, in his biography of the writer,* speaks of his "miscalculations about his own work" that were "part of his miscalculations about everything, including Italy and Europe":

> The poet William Jay Smith gives perhaps the fullest account of these latter. Lewis met Smith and his wife, Barbara Howes, and they invited him and Mrs. Powers to lunch at their villa, Il Fortino, high up on the Via del Pian' dei Giullari. He showed, they felt, a rather embarrassing sentimentality about Italy, and talked of the universal friendliness of the humble people, as if he felt that he were loved by everyone and that he could love everyone in turn. There was a good deal of talk about the "soul" of Europe, and the enrichment to Americans who could seize upon it. He himself discovered the embodiment of the "soul" of Europe that winter in a rather battered German blonde of indeterminate background and age who had been lurking about Florence for years and was known to nearly everyone as a tiresome cadger of drinks and meals. Entering a restaurant, willowy and apparently languid, her sharp eyes would sweep the place to discover the most likely touch, but, with her pretense to scholarship and her carefully managed mispronunciation of the right English words, she was for Lewis the vision of Europe, and he eagerly sought the enriching experience of buying her food and drink. He spoke excitedly of her to the Smiths.
>
> After that lunch, at which he admired their house and their view, he asked whether there were empty villas in the neighborhood. The establishment immediately below them, Villa La Costa, was available, as it usually was, since it had become a kind of joke among the Americans in Florence, being at once

*Sinclair Lewis: An American Life, by Mark Schorer (New York: McGraw Hill, 1961).

so ostentatious and impractical. Lewis expressed a wish to see it, and on the way back to Florence they stopped, found the caretaker and were shown around. Lewis thought it was lovely, but he said nothing more. In another year he would rent it, his last house, another embodiment of the "soul" of Italy for him, and as false, in fact, as the aging, begging blonde. (776–77)

I took Tom and Frank to visit this ostentatious dwelling, built in 1939 by some small Fascist official, which Schorer describes:

> Number 124, Villa La Costa, stands, like the others, behind its wall and closed gate, and presents not so much a formidable as a blank front, a glare of yellow plaster in the sunlight with eight or ten windows that seem small in such a long expanse, and an enormous arched oak door that the builder had appropriated, like a number of others in the house, from the storerooms of that great national monument in the city, the Palazzo Strozzi. Behind that door, the sight is assaulted by a glitter of marble, gilt, dead-white paint, glass, mirrors, crystal. In a foyer as large as a moderate-sized living room, dark-brown letters of marble laid in the beige marble of the floor spell out, at opposite ends of the area, two messages: *Pax et Bonum* and *Cor Tibi Pandit.*
> (785)

Tom loved it, more than anything else he saw that weekend, particularly the multi-colored intricate Venetian-glass banister that wound its way up the staircase that greeted them at the door.

Tom and Frank made their way back to Rome in their beautiful Buick on Monday, and the following morning I received an urgent telephone call from Frank. Tom had apparently left behind the manuscript of the play he was writing on the table in their room at the Hotel Berchielli. I retrieved it and sent it back to Rome. It was the first draft of the opening of *The Rose Tattoo*, which Tom dedicated to Frank for having introduced him to Sicily.

◆ ◆ ◆

Not long after Tom and Frank left, the owners of Il Fortino informed us that they needed it back and would not renew our lease. It was our great good fortune to locate immediately on the opposite side of the Arno in San Domenico just below Fiesole a residence far better than any we had dreamed of. It was the recently remodeled peasant house on the former estate of the English poet Walter Savage Landor. It offered, along with a superb view of the valley, affordable space and comfort. When our son David was born in August, we found a competent nanny to look after him and an excellent cook. There followed two of the most pleasant years I have spent anywhere on this planet. We were both able to write every day and meet some of the talented American writers and painters who then gathered in Florence just as their predecessors had in Paris after the First World War.

To help cover our expenses, I enrolled under the GI Bill at the University of Florence, and it was there in an Italian literature course that I met a young American writer, John Robinson, who had published stories in the *New Yorker* and *Horizon*. He had served in Italy with the American army, struggling against the Germans all the way up from Sicily, and had just returned on a Fulbright Fellowship to the country he had loved since he first set foot on it. He intended, we understood, to depict it in his fiction with the special appreciation that his war experience had given him. We found him to be a delightful companion with the charm, wry humor, and keen intelligence of the gifted Southern gentleman he was. He had grown up in Jackson, Mississippi, the son of a prominent Delta family, and his closest schoolmate had been the celebrated writer Eudora Welty. He sang her praises to such an extent whenever we saw him and spoke so frequently of their joyous times together before and after the war that we were convinced that she was much more than just a close classmate—she was clearly the love of his life. We had been Welty admirers for some time, and I was particularly thrilled to think that I would meet the author of *A Curtain of Green* (1941), a collection of stories as memorable and meaningful to me as Tom's play *The Glass Menagerie* (1945) had been. When Eudora did arrive, we were in London, where we had gone to see *A Streetcar Named Desire* directed by Lawrence Olivier and with Vivien Leigh in the role of Blanche DuBois.

We had expected to respond as favorably to the play as the New York audience had and were extremely disappointed that we did not. Barbara, a proper Bostonian, was not reacting as a number of her associates probably had to *Battle of Angels*, performed in Boston in 1940. She had spent some time in the South and was ready to join me in enthusiastically endorsing this work of the poet-playwright she had recently entertained. When our new friends came to greet us on our return to Florence, I felt certain that, as a fellow pioneering Southern writer, Eudora Welty would approve of the plays of Tennessee Williams. Ultimately she did in the strongest way, but just then, with that sparkle in her eye that soon became familiar, she said quietly but firmly that she had disliked this particular play when she saw it on Broadway, and John Robinson agreed with her. I thought that they both must have disapproved of the portrayal of Blanche DuBois, that lady from the Mississippi Delta, which they both knew so well. Eudora's *Delta Wedding* (1946) owed much to the diaries of John's grandmother.

That there may have been other reasons for her disapproval I discovered much later. She had attended the performance of *Streetcar* not with John Robinson, but with her agent Diarmuid Russell, who disliked intensely any sexual display on the stage, and his strong feeling may have influenced her. She was collaborating at this time with her friend Hildegard Dolson on a series of comic sketches for the theater and she wanted to do a parody of *Streetcar*. Dolson would not hear of it; to her there was nothing funny about that play.

One of the best reviews of *A Streetcar Named Desire* may explain both my disappointment and Eudora's disapproval. It was written by Kenneth Tynan, whom I had known at Oxford in 1947 before he began work as a theater critic in 1948. This section of his essay on the plays of Arthur Miller and Tennessee Williams (1954), because it is frequently overlooked, is worth quoting in its entirety:

> *You Touched Me!*, on which Williams collaborated with Donald Wyndham ... was followed in 1947 by *A Streetcar Named Desire*, which was directed by Kazan, who seems to have an instinct for the best of both Miller and Williams. It is perhaps the most misunderstood of his plays: the English and French productions were both so blatantly sensationalized that Williams' underlying lyric fibre passed unnoticed. If Willy Loman is the desperate average man, Blanche DuBois is the desperate exceptional woman. Willy's collapse began when his son walked into a hotel apartment and found him with a whore; Blanche's when she entered "a room that I thought was empty" and found her young husband embracing an older man. In each instance the play builds up to a climax involving guilt and concomitant disgust. Blanche, nervously boastful, lives in the leisured past; her defense against actuality is a sort of aristocratic *Bovarysme*, at which her brutish brother-in-law Stanley repeatedly sneers. Characteristically, Williams keeps his detachment and does not take sides: he never denies that Stanley's wife, in spite of her sexual enslavement, is happy and well-adjusted, nor does he exaggerate the cruelty with which Stanley reveals to Blanche's new suitor the secrets of her nymphomaniac past. The play's weakness lies in the fact that the leading role lends itself to grandiose overplaying by unintelligent actresses, who forget that when Blanche complains to her sister about Stanley's animalism, she is expressing, however faintly, an ideal:

> Such things as art—as poetry and music—such kinds of new light have come into the world since then! ... That we have got to make *grow*! And *cling* to, and hold as our flag! In this dark march toward whatever it is we're approaching ... Don't—don't hang back with the brutes!

When, finally, she is removed to the mental home, we should feel that a part of civilization is going with her. Where ancient drama teaches us to reach nobility by contemplation of what is noble, modern American drama conjures us to contemplate what might have been noble, but is now humiliated, ignoble in the sight of all but the compassionate.[3]

I wasn't sure that this review answered all the questions I had about the London performance, but the message of the play was certainly lost. It would be years before I could truly fathom the mystery of Streetcar, however it was performed. I did not at this time pursue the subject. We were soon totally involved in exploring the mystery of Florence with Eudora, who gave us a new vision and interpretation of every building, painting, and sculpture we examined. We took them both to meet some of the celebrated residents, Bernard Berenson, Harold Acton, and Francesco Guicciardini, and any number of American and English writers and painters who were just passing through. Barbara was then a part-time hostess at I Tatti, where she arranged a luncheon. The host Berenson found Eudora enchanting and maintained a correspondence with her for the rest of his life. We made many excursions outside the city, including a memorable one to Siena, and on all of them I became increasingly familiar with the character and personality of Eudora Welty and with many aspects of her phenomenal talent as a writer. Nine years older than I, she became for me during my entire literary life the kind of mentor that Tom Williams had been at the beginning.

During these happy weeks we had the impression that Eudora felt closer to John than she had in years. It led me to ask him why, in heaven's name, they hadn't yet got married. His answer was: "Oh, we love each other too much for that." A perplexing and not very promising response, I thought. At the end of March, Eudora left for a month in England and Ireland. Back in Italy in May, she was joined by her lifelong friend Dolly Wells. John accompanied them to Capri, Pompeii, and Rome. Then after a week on their own, they settled with him in a villa he had rented, a splendid mansion in the hills near Florence, with a garden, a swimming pool, and a fully equipped staff. (It had been rented the previous year by Dylan and Caitlin Thomas, and it was there that he wrote his poem "In Country Sleep.") John was pleased to be again the country gentleman he truly was, to pick his peaches and grapes, make his own wine, and serve Bourbon and Branch water to his guests. Eudora loved the setting, but occasionally she took Dolly into town.

One of the American writers she saw there was Truman Capote. Barbara and I were sitting one day with Eudora and her friend Dolly at Leland's Bar on the Via Tornabuoni when Truman, with his partner Jack Dunphy, came in. Before anyone could say anything, Truman hurled himself into Eudora's arms, saying, in a high shrill voice that resounded throughout the entire establishment, that she was a great writer and that it was the highpoint of his life to have this opportunity to say so to her face. I asked them both to join us, and, after they had each ordered a *sugo di pomodoro* (spicy tomato juice, Leland's specialty), Truman nodded briefly to all of us and fixed his whole attention on Eudora. Jack Dunphy recalled to Barbara and me the evening they had spent the year before with us and Tennessee Williams. He told Dolly how he wished that she and Eudora had been in Florence then, and went on to speak of his journey since with Truman to Ischia, Capri, Amalfi, and the south of Italy. Finally he turned to interrupt Truman and remind him of a luncheon engagement they had elsewhere.

After they had gone, Dolly sighed, as if relieved, and, gazing across the table, told Eudora that she wondered how in the world she could bear to speak to Truman Capote after he had stolen so much from her in his new novel *Other Voices, Other Rooms*, which had been highly praised by most critics.

"*Other Voices,*" Dolly said. "My foot! There sure were *other voices* in that book and the best of them were *yours*. Why, he lifted whole segments of dialogue, copied the action in many places, and even took the names of some of your characters. That's going a bit far, don't you think?"

"No, all that really doesn't bother me," Eudora said. "What's important is whether or not he has been true to his gift, to his talent, and I think he has. He *is* truly talented, and, as he moves on, he'll settle more clearly into his own style, and he'll go far."

I soon discovered that this was Eudora's way of judging a writer: whether or not he is being true to his talent. One who is not would, in his work, run off the rails and be quickly forgotten. I wondered if Eudora had ever thought of passing this judgment on John Robinson, the writer she loved passionately.

A year later, when she was in Ireland, on her second visit to Bowen's Court, the home of Elizabeth Bowen, who became a close friend, she spoke of John Robinson and his problems as a writer. The next day she sent him this note: "Last night Elizabeth was asking more about your writing & finally said maybe you hadn't discovered your subject perhaps? The one that *would have* you at work writing on it. She has instinct. Most gently & tentatively she was offering it & I pass it on for that." But in Florence she didn't discuss John's writing problems with him. He gave her and Dolly a lovely farewell party. Barbara and I drove them to Venice and stayed with them until early in June when they sailed for New York on the *Saturnia.*

Whether John ever answered Elizabeth Bowen's question I do not know, but Eudora continued to have high expectations for his career as a writer. In the spring of 1952 he was at Yaddo, the Writers' Colony in Saratoga Springs, New York, where he worked on a long story called "Coming of Spring" that he sent to her just before leaving. She was more severely critical of this story than of anything that he had written. The narrator is a nineteen-year-old man and his narrative concerns an older man, a painter Tom, and he seems unable to clarify the nature of Tom's relationship with his landlord and with Carl, who had been a nude model for one of his paintings. Eudora said, "You limit the point of view on purpose, and through this the story emerges confused and hectic and part of the scenery, as it were, the atmosphere and the tension altogether that of a love affair but never translatable to the narrator into the other things that most surely are there." What was clearly not translatable to the narrator but was perfectly translatable to the reader was that this all concerned a homosexual love affair.[4]

Eudora thought at once of the twenty-year-old Italian man, Enzo Rocchigiani, whom John, at forty-five, had taken with him to Mexico, and whom she had met on their return to New York. When she took the two of them to dinner with Dolly Wells, she realized for the first time that the two men were a couple. Because of visa difficulties, Enzo could not remain in New York as John had planned. When he returned to Italy, John left to join him there, where they would live together until John died. After reading the draft of "Coming of Spring," which John had written at Yaddo, Eudora wrote to him a second time, apologizing for having been so severe at first in her judgment. But from then on she wrote to him less often, and it was clear that the relationship would never be the same again.

Had John finally found his subject, which was homosexuality, but, having found it, been unable to write openly about it? And had Eudora ever asked herself if John had been true to his talent? If she had, she would have found, to her dismay, that he did not really possess the great talent that she always assumed he had. But Eudora could never accept the fact that her closest friend, whom she loved passionately, was not also a supremely gifted writer. They had grown up together, sharing and loving the same things, and writing was, for her at least, as natural as breathing. But John knew that he was not basically a writer, and when he found that he simply could not write, as much as he wanted to, he stopped. He devoted his life and his love to Italy, and to the young man who for him represented the very essence of it.

Years later in *Cat on a Hot Tin Roof* Eudora found that Tennessee Williams had imagined a character, Maggie, the Cat, who played on stage a role very similar to the one she had assumed in real life—that of a woman waiting in vain for the physical attention of the man she loved. When she reviewed the play, as we shall see, it was with the greatest appreciation and understanding.

7

With Williams at
a Performance of *America Hurrah*
by Jean-Claude van Itallie

I had married my French wife, Sonja Haussmann, in Paris in early September 1966, and she had come over to join me in November at Williamstown, Massachusetts, where I was teaching at Williams College. We had decided to spend the Christmas holidays in New York. I had had good reports of *America Hurrah*, which had opened in November at the Pocket Theatre on lower Third Avenue. I got tickets for the performance and we were not disappointed.

America Hurrah was a trilogy of one-act plays: *Interview*, *TV*, and *Motel* by Jean-Claude van Itallie. Born in Brussels in 1936 into a non-practicing Jewish family, he had fled with them from the Nazis, landing in New York City in late 1940. He had grown up in what he called the "death-denying suburb" of Great Neck, Long Island, and, speaking French at home and English at school, had developed a keen interest in words and learned early on that "reality is not contained in any single language." As a student at Harvard, he had been influenced by the avant-garde theater of Beckett, Ionesco, and Genêt in Paris and of Brecht in Germany. The films of Fellini, Antonioni, and Bergman had also prompted him to look with a fresh eye at the world immediately around him and at the intense social conflict that the Vietnam War had brought to a head.

Interview is a fugue for eight actors that begins and ends with the rhythmic continuing evocation of a group of applicants at an employment agency, all by the name of Smith.

TV dramatizes the degrading, trivializing power of the mass media in the viewing room of a television-rating studio. The television images break free of the set and gradually engulf the trio of on-stage viewers. What is forcefully presented is a close-up real view of the empty images that the American public is being offered endlessly every day.

Motel is a masque of three dolls, and the dolls for the original production were created by Robert Wilson, the first of many such puppets that he continued to create and that brought him world fame. The Midwestern Motel room in which the Motel-Keeping Doll stands is anonymously modern, except for certain "homey" touches. A neon light blinks outside the window. The colors in the room like the colors in the clothes of the Man and Woman Dolls are violent combinations of oranges, pinks, and reds, against a reflective plastic background.

Bill Coco describes the action of the play: "A larger-than-life Motel-Keeper Doll spews forth an increasingly staccato monologue about the room and its furnishings, which are the mail-order-catalogue surface of violent America. As she talks, the larger-than-life Man Doll and Woman Doll enter the motel room, scrawl graffiti on the walls, tear the room apart, tear the Motel-Keeper Doll apart, and march out through the audience, brandishing the Motel-Keeper's limbs, while a siren wails loudly."

The Motel-Keeper's Voice kept spewing out these words: Self-contained latrine waters, filters, counters, periscopes and mechanical doves, hooked rugs, dearest little picture frames for loved ones—made in Japan—through the catalogue. Cat-a-logue. You pick items and products cablecackles—so nice—cuticles, twice-twisted combs with corrugated calisthenics, meat-beaters, fish-tackles, bug bombs, toasted terra-cottad Tanganyikan switchblades, ochre closets, ping-pong balls, didies, Capricorn and Cancer prognostics, crackers, total uppers, stick pins, basting tacks.

As the siren continued to sound and the motel door opened and the car headlights shone into the eyes of the audience, I turned and stared straight across the aisle, and there, a broad smile on his face, was my friend Tom—Tennessee Williams—seated with his new friend Bill Galvin. I had been told that Tom was stoned in the sixties and so I was prepared for the fixed, stoned smile that indicated his absolute approval of these plays and all that they stood for.

Robert Brustein had written that with these three plays "the American theater takes three giant steps toward maturity . . . van Itallie has discovered the truest poetic function of the theatre . . . to invent metaphors which can poignantly suggest a nation's nightmares and afflictions." And Norman Mailer wrote, "It is possible *Motel* is the best one-act play I have ever seen." *America Hurrah* ran for two years here off-Broadway, then moved to the Royal Court Theatre in London, and was later acclaimed in Sydney, Australia, where the cheering audience formed a barricade to prevent the police from arresting the actors (because of the graffiti displayed in *Motel*).

We put our coats back on and, still beaming with satisfaction, made our way out of the theater.

We mumbled something to one another about stopping somewhere to have a drink, strolled out into the middle of Third Avenue, started walking north, with Tom and my wife, Sonja, leading the way. We walked for about a block when suddenly at the next street corner, from a bar on the right-hand side of the street, the body of a man who had been hit by another man literally flew through the air and fell at our feet. The violent male crowd poured immediately from the café right behind him and the brawl grew and continued. It was as if the scene that we had just seen enacted on stage before us was now continuing in the street. It spoke brilliantly of the message offered by van Itallie, which his colleague Tennessee Williams had resoundingly seconded, and actually all we could do then was hail a passing cab, get back to our hotel, and wonder about the world we were living in that we had seen so accurately and forcefully depicted for us that evening.

8

Reading of Williams
at Lynchburg College

In 1979 I was still teaching half the year at Hollins College, Roanoke, Virginia, when I heard that Tennessee Williams was to make an unusual three-day visit from September 23 to 25 at the central Virginia campus of Lynchburg College, which had held a month-long Tennessee Williams festival. There had been screenings of many of the films based on his plays, a Drama Department production of his *Summer and Smoke*, and assigned reading in all literature classes of his work. The highlight of his visit was to be an evening reading and commentary session in the college gymnasium that was open to the public. I decided to drive over and not miss this opportunity to hear him.

We met in the intervening years whenever possible. I regretted having had to miss his triumphant return in 1977 to Washington University, where he read his poems to a standing-room-only crowd in Graham Chapel. When asked about campus life in the 1930s, he told the interviewer for *Student Life* that he had "only the best of memories" of it and what he remembered most fondly was "the Poetry Club he belonged to." I met him numerous times at the American Academy and Institute of Arts and Letters, to which he brought once or twice his sister Rose. In 1975 when I was myself made a member of the Institute, I thanked him for whatever part he played in that election. He shook my hand, smiled, and said, "I voted for you."

When on December 3, 1976, the American Academy elected him a member, along with Elizabeth Bishop, Howard Nemerov, and John Updike, it held a luncheon afterward to which Institute members and guests were invited. I was delighted to attend with Sonja and to be seated at a table with him. I told him that I regretted as he did that our friend and associate Clark Mills had not continued to write poetry since he had started so brilliantly and had been such a guiding light for us. I agreed that Clark's translation of Rimbaud's poem "Bateau ivre" was the very best that had been done. I had not at that time read what he had written on the subject in his *Memoirs*, which had appeared the previous year. He had quoted one of the final stanzas of that translation from memory. I had looked up the original, published by Voyages Press, Ithaca, New York, in 1941:

> Of Europe's waters I seek none, except
> a cold black pool where one unhappy child
> kneels and releases towards the balm of dusk
> a boat frail as a butterfly in May.

In the last years of his life Williams often referred to Rimbaud, and the image of that unhappy child never left him.

What I did not tell Tom was that when Clark's lovely Filipina wife once served Sonja and me Sunday brunch in their Manhattan apartment on the southern tip of the island, Clark said that he had been trying with some difficulty to write about the St. Louis years. When he died, he left behind in his papers this account of the feeling of liberation and affection that he experienced, as did Tom, when they went to work together in the "literary factory" that they established in Clark's basement. How Tom would have welcomed these words set down carefully in jet-black ink on long legal pads!

Deep Well

Hard to believe the sight:
the water, welling straight
up from a deep spring,
pouring without a sound
near a big oak whose roots
had wound their way how far
down? Longer, I half guessed,
than I'd thought possible.
The charred walls, white clay
to pry loose, and with luck
switch off to carry home
and there prod into shape
warped ships and cats, the latter
changeable, in peculiar forms.
What I cannot forget and think
I shall not, is that water
welling, abundant, silent,
crystalline (I didn't know the word then)
as nothing I recall today
seeing or having heard of.
The water flowed up forever;
giving forever; clear, forever,
oh, far away from house
and mother, father, brother
bickering, shouting days on end.
It was a flowing, an abundance,
clear, a giving out of the earth
from forever to forever
oh, so far from mother, father, brother,
a world away from that house
locked like an attic box
where they shouted and argued

about what, brood as I might,
I never understood.
Later, there was the playground
by the old school of dark red brick
the whole in shadows. Islands
of sunlight shifted from place to place
on the hard-packed earth
as days and seasons came and went their way.
Oh, the flowing, the unbounded growing,
endless, abundant,
what was the word I had not
yet found? Affection, boundless, endless.

I remember very well why I was not present at the annual ceremonial of the American Academy and Institute of Arts and Letters
in 1969 when Williams was awarded the Institute's Gold Medal for
Drama. I was then consultant in poetry to the Library of Congress,
U.S. poet laureate, and the State Department had sent me on a two-
week cultural visit to Japan. I had perhaps been singled out for this
assignment because I had just published a book of poems, *The Tin
Can*, the title poem of which had an epigraph explaining that in Japan when a writer wants to get off to concentrate, it is said that he
or she has gone into the tin can (in Japanese the word is *kansume*).
This long poem explores the topic of private concentration literally
and figuratively in a very personal way. Copies of the book had been
sent ahead, one of them addressed to the novelist and dramatist
Yukio Mishima, whom I particularly wanted to meet. He invited
us—I was accompanied, of course, on this trip by my French wife—
to have drinks with him at the Empire Hotel shortly after we arrived. We were delighted that he would take the time involved away
from his own *kansume*. I conveyed to him a message from the lecture
agent Selma Warner to the effect that she would be pleased to offer
him the kind of profitable cross-country tour that she had arranged
for W. H. Auden, Andrei Voznesensky, and other famous writers.

His immediate witty dismissal of such a project led us on to a discussion of various aspects of the States that he remembered vividly from previous visits. In amazingly accurate and unaccented English, he continued to put to us both questions about what was happening culturally in New York and Paris. At the end of the hour he regretted to hear that we were leaving in two days for Osaka, Kyoto, and finally for the uppermost island Hokkaido and would not be back in Tokyo for another ten days.

On our return he said that he would like to invite us to the opening of his play *Madame de Sade* at one of the theaters with which he was associated. The next morning he dropped off at our hotel a copy of Donald Keene's English translation of the play so that we might familiarize ourselves with the text. As planned, later in May he sent his beautiful wife, Yoko, in her car to pick us up. With great pleasure we attended the opening and the reception that followed in a little underground theater. Then we went on to a far more elaborate and deeper underground establishment, Maxim's, the Tokyo version of the French restaurant. There, in a private room with their other guests, Edward Seidensticker, Mishima's translator, and Howard Hibbett, professor of Japanese at Harvard, we enjoyed a delicious dinner. It was accompanied by the best bread and wine we had had since Paris and a witty conversation on a variety of topics, mainly Japanese life, art and literature, past and present, with never anything remotely political. (Much of our host's life was indeed political: He had formed the Tatenokai [Society of the Shield], composed largely of students, in whom physically and emotionally he had instilled the ancient code of the samurai in protection, apparently, of a new emperor who would culturally embody the lost grandeur of Japan.) At the crack of dawn they drove us back to our hotel. "Au revoir," we said, expressing our desire to return one day their hospitality in New York or Paris. I was soon in bed with a little stack of Mishima's autographed books at my side, confident that I had met one the world's most gifted writers.

Little did we know that a few weeks after we departed, Tennessee Williams arrived. Crushed by the failure of his play, *In the Bar of a Tokyo Hotel*, and bitterly depressed by the articles in *Life* and the *New York Times* that pronounced him permanently finished as a writer, he had fled there, accompanied by Anne Meacham, who had played the lead in that brief production. He was warmly greeted by Yukio Mishima, who had been a friend and admirer of his work since their first meeting in the early 1950s in New York. He accomplished little, saw only the first act of the production of *A Streetcar Named Desire*, which had been long in preparation at the well-known Bungakuza Theatre, because illness forced him to leave. He suffered severely from the daily combined effect of drugs and alcohol. Mishima expressed his grave concern, fearing that his friend might well be on the edge of a total mental breakdown. In early July Williams returned to Key West for a restful ten days. Then, with his friend Bill Glavin, he flew to San Francisco and New Orleans, all the while more dependent on drugs and increasingly paranoid.

In mid-September, back in Key West he was preparing one morning a pot of coffee in his newly equipped kitchen. Lifting the pot from the stove, he tripped and fell, scalding his shoulder with hot coffee. He finally decided that he desperately needed help and not just for someone to convey him immediately to the cemetery as he had at first thought would be necessary. His brother Dakin, who came at once, managed to convince Tennessee that he should return to St. Louis and commit himself to Barnes Hospital, which they both knew from their boyhood as one of the foremost in the country. He was placed there in the mental ward, and in the course of the total—"cold turkey"—withdrawal from drugs, he suffered seizures and two heart attacks and was at first not expected to survive. By December, however, Tennessee was in better shape than he had been for years, but he could never accept the fact that Dakin had saved his life. He lived fourteen years longer, but never forgave his brother. Dakin, he claimed, had locked him up in the loony bin in order to finish him off and inherit his money. Although Dakin saw his brother numerous times during the following years, relations between them, which were not very good to begin with, never improved. When Tennessee died, Dakin was left out of the will.

A college gymnasium, I knew well from my own personal experience, is not the most agreeable place for a writer to speak, especially if the writer is a poet who plans to read and discuss poems. I entered this vast bleak area at Lynchburg College, every dark corner of which had been brightly lit to accommodate the audience of some 2,300 people who would assemble there, and found my way to a seat in the third row to the right of the platform.

After the college president's deep-throated, extended hyperbolic introduction, followed by applause that resounded from the rafters, Williams walked to the podium, paused, then, crooking his neck over the side, apologized for not having much of a voice with which to offer the poems that he planned to read. Reaching down inside the podium to fetch a bottle of red wine that he held high above his head, he announced proudly: "This little gift from one of the more decadent members of the English Department should help."

He then poured himself a glass that he lifted to toast the audience: "Here's to you, ladies and gentlemen," which brought forth a further roar of approval.

He proceeded to read several poems that deal powerfully with old age and madness, but rendered in the slurred, gnarled, and broken manner assumed that evening, he led his listeners on and on into a tangled verbal thicket in which they were totally lost. He then brought forth a copy of the novella, *The Knightly Quest*, spelled out the first word of the title, K-N-I-G-H-T-L-Y, and proclaimed that this was the best piece of cadenced prose he had ever written and it would sound very much like poetry. The words thickened, meaningless as they tumbled forth, and his listeners were relieved when he suddenly stopped, put down the book, and said that he would be happy to answer any questions except how he got the name Tennessee.

He completed this interrogation period quickly and announced that he would read a poem by his favorite poet, Hart Crane, who frequently went to the bars on the Brooklyn waterfront. The poem he had chosen, "Cutty Sark," was about one of his encounters there. "This poem," he said, "is supposed to be read when you are slightly inebriated, which, in this case, will be to my advantage."

It was painful for me to sit through an evening like this listening to a poet I had heard many times years before read with all the resonance and dramatic intensity that he expected of the actors in his plays.

After he had completed the reading, he nodded to accept the thundering applause. Then he wobbled, bowing of necessity from time to time briefly and rather gracefully and still smiling broadly, to the end of the platform, a few feet up the aisle on the far right from where I sat. A highly vocal and enthusiastic group of students, male and female, arrayed in an assortment of the rather peculiar get-ups that current college taste had dictated, quickly assembled around him. These were the active, energetic, extroverted young Virginia intellectuals who would, no doubt, the following week, tightly pack the hard sun-swept benches of the local football stadium. Tennessee greeted everyone warmly, cackling contently as he answered in a word or two an extended somber heart-felt and intricately pondered question concerning an early scene in *Summer and Smoke*, which the campus theater had produced and which had been required reading for a good portion of the student body. Turning then from the questioner, he had lifted his pen high in the air and brought it down quickly to rest bird-like on the extended open page of a volume of his plays and there scratched out precipitously his welcome but indecipherable signature.

A little coterie had gathered around Tennessee's traveling companion—Robert Carroll, I believe it was—on the side. Tennessee, glancing in their direction, broke off from his group and worked his way across to join them. He opened a door at the center of the wall behind them, explaining that the English Department had told him he could gather there with his friends. He ushered us all in to a long table, placed Carroll at one end, two of the coterie on each side, with himself at the other end and me beside him. I could see at once when the members of the coterie spoke up that they knew the playwright solely from his television appearances and that they had come to pick up and carry back whatever sexual tidbit the charming little guy would throw them. Tennessee gave them exactly what they had hoped for: a long tale of the complex intricate homosexual entanglements of four people, two male and two female. When he finished, they roared with laughter on both sides of the table. He had told a similar story when he accepted from Lillian Hellman the Gold Medal of Drama awarded to him by the National Institute of Arts and Letters. His listeners on that occasion did not find his account the least bit funny. It was for them, as this one was for me, a very bad parody of a serious play that he might one day write, if he had not already written it.

After a pause, Tennessee turned to me: "Tell us, Bill," he said, "about our life in St. Louis in the 1930s."

I was totally flustered, and stumbled "I—I remember you marching on the campus in your ROTC uniform."

I knew at once what a gaffe I'd made. I'd been thinking, of course, of brother Dakin: Tennessee corrected me. "I'll tell you," he said, "I certainly did wear the ROTC uniform but that was at the University of Missouri."

ROTC was required of all male students there only during their first two years. In the third year of training, which his father had insisted he take, that meant two classes a week in military science and a parade every Wednesday afternoon on the quadrangle. Students for those parades were required to put on a blue coat with white trousers. Thomas Lanier Williams, as he was then, must have looked a little strange on those days when the others marched in white trousers and he mistakenly, somewhere at the center, in blue ones—a blue joker in a steadily shuffled deck of crisp white playing cards.

He reminded us that he had been absent-minded in a similar way when he failed to pack the proper trousers before leaving for Lynchburg.

"I forgot the pants that go with this jacket," he told his audience during his reading this evening.

He then asked what I had been up to recently. I said that I had been revising a play that I had written some twenty years ago. I had received one of the Ford grants awarded in the early 1960s to poets and fiction writers to encourage them to write for the theater. My play, *The Straw Market*, had been composed and given a staged reading during the year I spent at Arena Stage in Washington, D.C.

A satire of the Americans who flocked to Florence after World War II, it deals with a Fulbright scholar, a young art critic, who, overcome by the beauty of the city, loses his heart and all his money to some beautiful but phony Florentine aristocrats. I told my friend Tom that he would surely recognize some of my characters based on people whom he met when he and Frank Merlo came in 1949 to visit me in Florence. (Edwin Sherin, who had been director at Arena Stage when I was there and had recently directed several plays by Tennessee Williams that met with his approval, had praised *The Straw Market* highly.) The play was first produced in 1961 at Hollins College, Virginia, where I had returned to teach. Harold Stone of the Julliard School in New York came down to direct it. Eleanor Wilson, a Hollins alumna who played a leading role with Tallulah Bankhead in the English version of Jean Cocteau's *The Eagle Has Two Heads*, came back to the campus to take the two leading female roles. Tom Ligon, who had played Billy Budd at Arena Stage, did a brilliant job as the Fulbright scholar.

The play had a staged reading the following year at the Poetry Center of the YMHA in New York with a group of top actors, the only play given such treatment since *Under Milk Wood* by Dylan Thomas. Agents in New York and London tried to find a place for it, but all the possible takers declined, saying that there were too many characters involved.

When we said good-bye that night, my friend Tom told me to be sure to send the play on to him. I did as he said, and, in a letter drafted to accompany it, wrote: "As you will see, it is very much a poet's play and is filled with poems and songs. I even wrote the music to the songs—very simple Calypso-type talk songs. It may now seem a period piece, but maybe not since it deals with the eternal theme of innocents abroad. I hope that it will amuse you."

I should have added a word about how much I had learned from reading and watching his plays over the years and how much I valued the example he had set early on of the hard and constant work it took to produce results of true artistic value.

In autumn 1959, on his way around the world with Frank Merlo, Tennessee Williams had spent two weeks in Tokyo and had seen much more of Yukio Mishima, who had introduced him to the Japanese theater. As a result of this visit, Tennessee had written a play, *The Day on Which a Man Dies: An Occidental Noh Play*, dedicated to his Japanese friend.

On May 8, 1960, back from his world tour in Key West, Williams confronted Mishima again but this time when interviewed by Edward R. Murrow from New York on his CBS television program. The two were joined from London by Dilys Powell, dean of the English film critics, and they plunged at once into a discussion of the plays and films of the two dramatists. Miss Powell remarked that she was interested in the treatment of love in the film of Mishima's novel *Conflagration* when the boy destroys the temple because he loved it so much. She felt that an "ordinary European audience" was often baffled by the complicated "modes of expression and thought" in Japanese films. At this point Tennessee remarked: "Miss Powell, you have to be a decadent Southerner to understand the Japanese cinema."

Because of its recent impact on an important theatrical event, let me quote verbatim a brief passage from this interview:

> YM: Miss Powell, I think a characteristic of Japanese character is just this mixture of very brutal things and elegance. It's a very strange mixture.
>
> TW: Yukio, about brutality and elegance: I think I understand what you mean. I'm not being snobbish when I say that, but I think you in Japan are close to us in the southern states of the United States.
>
> YM: I think so.
>
> TW: And I think I am able to understand how you could put those two terms together, brutality and elegance. I could not define why.
>
> YM: And I couldn't say why, either, but it is why I feel sympathy toward your work. I find our same characteristic mixture in your works, in your plays. For instance, *Suddenly Last Summer*, I think, is the most representative mixture of brutality and elegance.[1]

This dialogue was quoted in a February 2011 press release from the Comédie-Française in Paris announcing that it had chosen the first American play that it would perform since it was founded by royal edict in 1680. The play was *A Streetcar Named Desire* by Tennessee Williams. Muriel Mayette, the first woman to hold the powerful position of administrator of the troupe, said that she had proposed the staging of *Streetcar* because "Williams is now recognized in our universe and imagination as an important author who has influenced film and 20th-century theater with his exploration of class differences."

The play, in a new French translation, would run from March 5 to June 2, and to direct it Ms. Mayette had picked Lee Breuer. She remembered vividly seeing his production of a Samuel Beckett play in New York when she was sixteen years old and had followed his innovative international career ever since.

Breuer said, "We needed a metaphor for the South, but a south that makes sense with French cultural context. This play has been dominated by Elia Kazan's concept of how to stage it for 63 years. So why not try something different? A Japanese Orientalist style was not so distant from the faux aristocratic style of a Southern belle and it was popular in Paris."

With the assistance of his designer and artistic collaborator, Basil Twist, Breuer created a fantasy Japanese world with a modern and cinematographic use of the sliding screens that had originated in the sixteenth century on the island of Awajishima. Their painted scenes, alternately figurative and abstract, reflected the changing moods and actions on stage. Masked kurogo figures in black handled the props, all to the New Orleans jazz arranged by the composer John Margolis. I was eager to see how all these elements might be brought successfully together.

I attended a dress rehearsal of *Un Tramway Nommé Désir* in the red and gold Salle Richelieu of the Comédie-Française on March 4, 2011, and returned a month later for a second performance. My conclusion is that the director, Lee Breuer, himself a poet, has given us a truly visual poem. In its Japanese metaphorical transformation, it evokes magnificently the mad antebellum dream of Blanche DuBois. But for all the admirable dramatic and visual attention to brutality and elegance, it has turned a simple lyrical text into a grand operatic one and, in so doing, has lost the direct poetic message that Tennessee Williams clearly intended.

On September 30, 1970, Tennessee Williams, with his friend Oliver Evans, arrived on board the *President Cleveland* at the Port of Yokohama. As soon as they went ashore, where they were to spend three days, Tennessee called his friend Yukio Mishima, who said that he would be delighted to come from Tokyo the next day to see them. He arrived in the late afternoon, joined them for drinks in the hotel bar, then took them to dine in an immense red and gold Chinese restaurant. The headwaiter there, glancing quickly at Mishima, led them to an appropriate table and handed them an enormous menu. Tennessee asked for the wine list, ordered a bottle of Château Mouton-Rothschild, and, when they had all selected their dishes, turned to Mishima and asked what he was working on at the moment.

"I'm just finishing a novel," he said, "The last one in a tetralogy. What about you?"

"Revising a full-length play. I call it *The Two-Character Play.* Probably my last one. I don't have the energy to sustain a major work. It takes too much out of me. I intend to do short things from now on, and poems. I've done quite a few poems lately. But not another full-length play, no. It's too exhausting."

Back in Toyko, Mishima called to say that he would be pleased to obtain tickets for the Noh play that Tennessee wanted particularly to see. But unfortunately that would not be possible for the Americans: the play did not open until October 4, the very day that their ship was scheduled to depart for Hong Kong and Bangkok.

Around the time in September 1970 when Williams and Mishima met in Yokohama, I spoke, as one of the directors, along with Professor Frank MacShane of the Translation Center at Columbia University in New York, to a group of interested fiction writers, poets, dramatists, and professors on an important, but frequently neglected, subject, the art of literary translation. In the course of my remarks, I mentioned my visit the previous year to Tokyo, where Yukio Mishima had brought my wife and me a copy of Donald Keene's superb translation of his *Madame de Sade* so that we might familiarize ourselves with the play before we attended the opening of it, to which he had invited us.

Among the other speakers were Jacques Barzun, provost of the University, and the poet Stephen Spender. I believe that Donald Keene, professor of Japanese at Columbia, was also there, but because he spends at least half of each year in Japan, he may have been away. In any case, I remember telling him of my admiration for this work. It seemed to me nothing less that miraculous that he had been able to find, as professors of the language all testified, an English style that approximated that of one of the greatest stylists then writing in Japan. My thoughts that morning were certainly of him and of the writer who had so benefited from his artistic endeavor.

On November 25, 1970, Yukio Mishima assembled his Society of the Shield at the Tokyo headquarters of Japan's Self-Defense Forces, barricaded the office of the commandant, and tied him to his chair. He then went to the balcony, where he addressed the soldiers who had gathered below, intending to inspire a coup d'état that would restore the lost powers of the emperor. When the crowd merely scoffed and jeered at him, he went back inside, committed seppuku, and was himself beheaded.

When the news of this event reached Tennessee Williams and Oliver Evans in Bangkok, Evans was horrified but Williams was not surprised. He said later, as many other writers did, that Mishima had decided that with the final novel of his tetralogy, *Sea of Fertility*, he had completed his life's work as an artist and was ready to confront the "great mystery" of death.

As for me, I had expected Mishima one day to commit suicide, as his mentor Kawabata had done, but not at the early age of forty-five, and I did not believe that he would follow literally the code of the samurai, but so he did. Days before taking his life, he said in a letter to his friend and translator Donald Keene: "I am sure that you understand the actions I am about to perform, so I will not say anything about them. I have long thought that I wanted to die not as an author but as a military man."

9

Clothes for a Summer Hotel

Clothes for a Summer Hotel was the last of Tennessee Williams's plays to be presented on Broadway. It opened at the Cort Theatre in New York on March 26, 1980, his sixty-ninth birthday. I was pleased to be able to attend this production, and for the opening, in a telegram, I sent him this little verse:

> When at sixty-nine
> You can lay it on the line
> And write so well
> Of the living hell
> Of Zelda's hotel,
> Then your future looks bright—
> Good luck tonight.

> With memories of old times,
> Best wishes, Bill

But luck was not with him and one of the most interesting of Tom's plays did not receive the success it deserved.

At the end of January the play, directed by José Quintero, opened at the Eisenhower Theatre in Washington. The response was totally negative, but when it moved to Chicago in February producer Elliott Martin recalled that things looked very much better:

Williams's brother Dakin came to opening night with a big crowd of well-wishers, and Tennessee agreed to make more cuts. He worked closely with the cast, we had a good notice from Claudia Cassidy, and by the time we were ready to move to Broadway we all had a false sense of security. . . back in New York we still had a fighting chance, but then the blizzard of 1980 came and, on top of that a transit strike . . . the audience was really ecstatic about the play, but the critics were not and the weather and the transit strike finalized the decision. We had to close the show on April 16th. All plays did badly that season, but especially plays like ours which had every problem well documented in the press during rehearsals and the out-of-town run.[1]

"This is a ghost play," the author tells us in an introductory note and adds immediately, "of course, in a sense all plays are ghost plays, since players are not actually whom they play.

"Our reason for taking extraordinary license with time and place is that in an asylum and on its grounds liberties of this kind are quite prevalent: and also these liberties allow us to explore in more depth what we believe is truth of character.

"And so we ask you to indulge us with the license we take for a purpose which we consider quite earnest."[2]

The liberties permit the characters to represent their former selves but also other characters living and dead. Thus Zelda also represents Rose, the author's sister; and Zelda's husband, as Scott Fitzgerald, represents at the same time another author, Tennessee Williams himself, who has on occasion followed Fitzgerald from reality to the make-believe world of Hollywood.

This is one of the most poetic of Williams's plays and also one of the most Shakespearean. The characters are indeed ghosts who move on and off stage as they do in Shakespeare, occupying a different time and place and on occasion a different character. The ghosts come in pairs—Zelda and Rose, Scott and Tennessee, Scott and Hemingway, who also become Tennessee and Hemingway and at times Tennessee and himself. This is the most objective of Tennessee's plays but at the same time the most personal. From beginning to end it is all metaphor: as spectators we are in the barred world of madness, a world that sits upon a windy hilltop so that it may receive fully the free-moving and omnipresent, unimpeded spirit of poetry. The characters cross and re-cross as in the Noh dramas that Williams has studied, shifting screens that shade them as they are taken from dream to reality and back again. The whole is the ballet governed by Zelda's rhythmic voice: *un deux, pliez, un deux, pliez, etc.*, the dark sleeves of the Catholic sisters' habits assist in shifting the action through time and space. The intern working at the asylum is also the aviator who is Zelda's lover, representative of the freedom that she constantly demands. There are so many examples of these poetically just turns and situations that I could go on listing them for pages and still not touch all that brilliantly holds this drama together.

All of the plays of Tennessee Williams are about light and dark, but here the degrees of *chiaroscuro*, light and shadow, are so multiple and intense that it is no wonder that most of the New York critics missed them.

The title prepares us for the poetry of the play with its many levels of meaning. The leading male character arrives dressed for a summer hotel, but he finds a southern asylum in a cold windy setting that requires darker heavier clothing to cover the light and summery aspect of everything.

From the very beginning of this work Tennessee Williams contrasts the "cheerful idiocy of noon," the normal world in which most of us live, with the dark, vaulted nightmare world of the soul, the "beanstalk country" that the mad inhabit and that is unknown to us. This contrast is made clear in this fine early poem:

The Beanstalk Country

You know how the mad come into a room,
too boldly,
their eyes exploding on the air like roses,
their entrances from space we never entered.
They're always attended by someone small and friendly
who goes between their awful world and ours
as though explaining but really only smiling,
a snowy gull that dips above a wreck.

They see not us, nor any Sunday caller
among the geraniums and wicker chairs,
for they are Jacks who climb the beanstalk country,
a place of hammers and tremendous beams,
compared to which the glassed solarium
on which we rise to greet them has no light.

The news we bring them, common, reassuring,
drenched with the cheerful idiocy of noon,
cannot compete with what they have to tell
of what they saw through cracks in the ogre's oven.

And we draw back. The snowy someone says,
Don't mind their talk, they are disturbed today![3]

The play reflects Tom's early visits to the asylum residence of Rose
and to the later asylum interior to which his brother relegated him.

The "snowy gull that dips above a wreck" in the poem is echoed
in the "idiotically cheerful white-starched nurse" who wheels the patient Boo-Boo up to her roommate Zelda, and when Zelda realizes
she cannot receive the audience into her haunted world, she offers
them "a polite social smile and a slight bow." What an elegant gesture

this is beside the vulgar wheeling of the "snowy gull" above the abandoned wreck. The play's action is summed up in Zelda's speech:

> Sunset Hill on which this cage is erected is the highest to catch
> the most wind to whip the flame-like skirts as red as the sisters'
> skirts are black. Isn't that why you selected this place for my
> confinement?

The action moves always between red and black, between the purifying dazzle of fire and the black indistinguishable ash that will remain when fire sweeps through the asylum, as Zelda knows it will.

> "I am not a salamander do you hear?" she asks. "You've mis-
> taken my spirit for my body. Because my spirit exists in fire
> does not mean that my body will not be consumed if caught in
> fire behind barred gates and windows on this windy hill."

The salamander is that lizard-like mythical creature that is capable of surviving in fire. It often became the emblem for the endurance of nobility.

The playwright presents madness that is purified by the inspiring flame that every artist attempts to approach as close as possible but which, because of the discipline that art demands, can never be allowed to both consume and purify him or her at the same time.

Zelda clearly wants to have both the madness that she naturally possesses and the madness of art that she thinks she merits more than her husband. Tennessee Williams appears to agree with her and with the doctor who finds that Zelda's writing is at times superior and more imaginative than her husband's.

> "The incredible things are the only true things, Scott," Zelda
> tells him. "You don't dare admit that you know that to exist is
> the original and greatest of incredible things. Between the first

wail of an infant and the last gasp of a dying man—it's all an arranged pattern of submission to what's been prescribed for us unless we escape into madness or into acts of creation."

Escape into the acts of creation, according to Fitzgerald and Hemingway, is with discipline possible. Tennessee Williams seems to wish like Zelda to escape into both madness and creation. It was only when he was drunk or drugged, we are told, that he put on a wig in a bar and pretended actually to be Rose, but fundamentally he knew that she could not share with him, nor could he with her, the results of his escape into creation, which was achieved by long hours of hard work at his desk. Still, in real life, after this play Tennessee wanted to maintain a link with the mad woman he loved. The play ends with Scott insisting that Zelda accept from him a ring as an emblem and reminder of their life together. Similarly, just after the close of this play Tennessee purchased for Rose a beautiful ring which delighted her and which she would retain and would not return as she had the previous little jade ring that he had given her. When Rose returned that ring, he gave it to Carson McCullers, one of the other women who had played an important role in his life.

I should like to conclude with a poem of my own related to Scott Fitzgerald and the 1920s. Harry Crosby was a wealthy American friend whom he and Zelda frequently saw in Paris. He was a dilettante but his poems and journals are not without interest. He literally worshiped what he termed the Black Sun, and this fact, as well as the circumstances of his fast life and strange death, seems to have been on Fitzgerald's mind when he wrote *The Great Gatsby*. Crosby was found dead one morning in a hotel room beside his mistress. They had painted the bottoms of their feet black, and he had shot her and himself.

His widow, Caresse Crosby, speaks in her autobiography of the former mill on the outskirts of Paris where Harry used to play *Petits Chevaux* with his friends—those lead or wooden horses that you move along the floor usually on shipboard. He had devised what he called the Bedroom Stakes and had given the horses names such as Fidelity, Frivolity, and Concubine.

Petits Chevaux: The Twenties

I

Harry Crosby one day launched the Bedroom Stakes—
Frivolity out in front, Fidelity overtaken by Concubine.
The play was fast, the bets were high. Who lost? Who won?
Green baize drank the tilting shadows of the sun,
And Death left the players' goblets brimming with blood-red wine.

II

Scott Fitzgerald organized the Crack-up Stakes—
The horses galloped ahead; Victrola records turned.
He downed his drink and wrote; wife Zelda whirled and swayed;
The goblets shattered, but the words survived Time's raid,
And Zelda danced on madly till the asylum burned.

10

Award of Medal of Freedom to Williams by President Carter

On June 9, 1980, President Jimmy Carter presented the Medal of Freedom to Admiral Hyman G. Rickover and to thirteen other distinguished Americans. The admiral had been the mentor of the president and the father of the nuclear U.S. Navy. Among the others who were honored were Beverly Sills, the opera singer; Ansel Adams, the photographer; and the late John Wayne, the actor. It was fitting that President Carter, as a Southern president, had chosen three Southern writers to honor, Eudora Welty, Robert Penn Warren, and Tennessee Williams. Eudora had invited Sonja and me, along with Reynolds Price, Rosie Russell, Charlotte Capers, John and Catherine Prince, and Walter Clemons, to be her guests on this occasion. For me this was a very special day—not only were these three great Southerners, they had also been my close friends for many years, and so I felt that my entire extended Southern and intellectual family was being brought together for this event. (In the case of Tennessee Williams, it was not just our early friendship that united us. He had planned, in 1948, to write a play about Huey Long tentatively called "The Big Time Operators." In it he pictured Huey Long very sympathetically as really close to the people but shackled by a corrupt party boss. He portrayed Long in his late twenties when he had just been elected governor. Tom did not know at this time that my father had taken me, a twelve-year-old boy, to meet Huey, his former neighbor and best friend, but this fact made Tom, on this day, an even more intimate member of my imagined, extended Southern family.)

In a letter to Mary Louise Aswell, Eudora described the occasion:

It was a bright, absolutely cloudless, refreshingly cool day in Washington, and the medal giving was outdoors, in the back part of the lawn down those circular steps at the back of the White House that you know from the newsreels. The Marine Band played, our guests were seated on chairs in the shade facing a little low platform, and we came forward in alphabetical order—(you know where I came—between Robert Penn Warren and in front of Tennessee Williams [the end])—each of us escorted by a young Marine aide that wasn't going to let us fall down. Then (we were all announced as we approached) just at the last minute another W was inserted between Red and me—turned out to be Mrs. John Wayne, a little late in getting there from California but the only lady with a hat, all in white, her hat was a cartwheel; and she was very dark, Spanish.[1]

The cartwheel hat, being black, assumed an even greater prominence.

While they were all standing there, Eudora told us that Tom had asked her, "Where do you live, Miss Welty?" That was clearly a nervous question. He knew very well, as did her other thousands of readers, that she lived in Jackson, Mississippi, a city that she had made famous throughout the world.

I remembered Tom's having remarked once at Washington University that it would be impossible to gain recognition as a Southern writer because, in addition to William Faulkner, all attention was already focused on Eudora Welty and Katherine Anne Porter.

Eudora told us later at the table that a fly had landed on Tennessee's cheek and then had circled his head for several minutes.

I thought of the many houseflies that had pursued Tom in his long career. When he gave Maria St. Just a copy of *Battle of Angels*, he told her that reading the play, she should think of him writing it, "creeping and crawling" in the attic of Clayton, Missouri, feeling "as wretched as ten flies at the end of summer." And I recalled as well the troubling flies that kept buzzing around Emily Dickinson as she composed the many memorable poems that he loved to quote. But Eudora Welty, being the great storyteller that she was, immediately followed up her mention of Tom's winged tormentor with the description of a Mississippi fly that was said to have perched one day on a prominent state politician. The latter's eyes, she told us, were so close together that if the fly had landed on his nose it would have had one foot in one eye and one in the other. She had us all roaring with laughter.

Of what went on at the Williams table we have no report. His agent, Mitch Douglas, said that Tennessee's mother had died a week earlier at the age of ninety-five but that he had seemed to put that event behind him and to be looking forward to the White House ceremony. The only difficulty, Mitch said, was that Tennessee at the very last minute wanted to include someone who had just showed up—Schuyler something—whose name had not been on the list of guests submitted in advance. He was dragged along anyway and was miraculously admitted. When Tennessee wanted to, Mitch said, he could be the gentleman of the world, as he was that day at the White House, when he finally got there.

In a letter to Reynolds Price, Eudora Welty in May 1955 had discussed her response to *Cat on a Hot Tin Roof* by Tennessee Williams, which she had just seen in the New York production directed by Elia Kazan with Burl Ives, Barbara Bel Geddes, and Ben Gazzara in the leading roles: "I had to take back everything I was mad at Tennessee Williams about—for this play seemed honest, serious, about something (this is like the 'goal' in that Chekhov letter, a little) and a good use of all that material he sometimes seemed to me to just fling about like a child with a dollar's worth of fire-crackers."[2] She expanded on her view of *Cat on a Hot Tin Roof* in the program notes she wrote in *The Spotlight* for the play's performance, directed by her friend Frank Hains at the Jackson Little Theater, February 2–10, 1959. These program notes, which speak with great brilliance about the play, are reprinted here in their entirety:

Mr. Williams' plays burst in on us with such extraordinary voltage that—just as after a crisis in real life—we find it hard to describe afterwards what hit us. Was it violence or excruciating tenderness, that sharpest moment? Was it unbearable crudeness or extraordinary delicacy that finally drove the point home? Have all our senses just been impaled on some hopeless reality, or are we arguing with a dream? And wasn't it beautiful when the whole Delta, surely the whole world outside, seemed to stop and listen while the mockingbird sang?

Brilliant as Tennessee Williams' technical endowment is, aren't we convinced by the time the curtain falls that an even greater power lies in something within, in his driving wish to show us something about ourselves? Behind every play he's written we seem to hear crying out a belief that as human beings we don't go so far—no matter how far we do go—as to tell each other the truth.

We see his characters living without honor, or in nothing but a dream of honor, haunted by the past, wrenched by the present, blind to the future. We hear them yell and holler and rave into each other's faces, or wait while they reach out in silence toward each other—they never crash the sound barrier of understanding.

The brutality of some of his characters, no less than the dreaming of others, must be a cloak to hide the truth from themselves and one another. The reason is (he seems to be saying) that out of ignorance, wrongheadedness, pride, desire, rage, despair, perversity, or just plain fuzziness—and often in spite of love—we don't know how to communicate.

"Mendacity?" pipes up Sister Woman, after Big Daddy's most searing speech. "Big Daddy, I'm afraid I don't know what that word means."

In the North, so we hear, they don't believe people talk like this. In the South we know people talk like this, and because we can recognize so much—of speech, place, character, life—might we run the risk of missing something else?

Not when we really look and listen at this play—that, bringing so much familiarity home, is as full of strange and wonderful and thought-provoking things as if it were written by some visitor foreign to our shores, who has come here and cast his eyes upon us. Indeed it is the eye of a poet.[3]

I find it valuable, I believe, to follow Eudora Welty's notes with what Tennessee Williams himself wrote about his own play:

Much has been made in recent months of the fact that this year (1972) marks the silver anniversary of *A Streetcar Named Desire* which most people interested in my writing still regard as my best work for the theater. I am more inclined to *Cat on a Hot Tin Roof*, that is, toward the play in its original and true form without the anticlimactic reappearance of Big Daddy in Act Three, with nothing to do but tell an off-color story about a male elephant being visibly influenced by the seasonal aura of a female elephant in the adjoining stall.

With that gratuitous bit eliminated from the play, along with the ingenuous solution of the marital dilemma between Maggie and Brick, I feel that with this play of 1954–55 I went far as I was ever likely to go in my career as a playwright toward the mastery of that profession: It had a fairly large group of characters most of whom were created "in depth," as they say, and the remainder with sufficiently accurate detail, and the play ran without interruption in time for the exact course in which the curtain was up. And it was based upon what I believe to be the most important theme that I have essayed in my writing for the theater: the mendacity that underlies the thinking and feeling of our affluent society.

11

Death of Tennessee Williams

I had arrived early at the Frank E. Campbell Funeral Home on Madison Avenue on Sunday morning, February 27, 1983, to view the closed coffin of my friend Tom. I was living then on the twentieth floor of a rent-subsidized apartment on York Avenue between Eighty-Seventh and Eighty-Eighth Streets and gazed at length at dawn that day out over the East River toward the Triborough Bridge and thought how much Tom loved the morning light that he would never see again. He had died on Friday at the Hotel Elysée at 60 East Fifty-Fourth Street, "that shrine," he had told me, "to many old actresses such as Ethel Barrymore, Tallulah Bankhead, Dorothy Gish," although he wasn't sure that glorious Millay had ever hung her harp there.

The New York medical examiner had at first reported that the poet-playwright had choked to death on a plastic medicine bottle cap, but months later issued a second report stating that the laboratory had found he had overdosed on barbiturates.

The complete story about this did not come out until six years later. Then Dr. Michael M. Baden, who had preceded Elliot Gross as New York medical examiner, explained exactly what had happened:

> Gross found a long, thin rubber bottle stopper in his mouth
> and attributed his death to it: Williams choked on it, he said.
> However, it was not wide enough to stop up Williams's airway.
> In fact, it was not even *in* his airway. It was in his mouth. He
> had been drinking and had overdosed on barbiturates. The

press kept calling Gross for the toxicology report, and he kept saying the work wasn't done yet. . . . Six months later, after the press had lost interest, Gross quietly issued another cause of death, taking into account the secret toxicology findings—that Williams had swallowed enough barbiturates to cause death.*

I like to think that the "rubber bottle stopper" was from a bottle of liquid used for eye treatment and that his last breath would have been trying to soothe the eyes that had always given him such trouble and which, as he had said in an early poem, are always "last to go out":

The eyes are not lucky.
They seem to be hopelessly inclined to linger.

They make additions that come to no final sum.
It is really hard to say if their dark is worse than their light,
Their discoveries better or worse than not knowing.

But they are last to go out,
And their going out is always when they are lifted.

I remembered the line of Rilke that he had chosen as an epigraph for his *Summer and Smoke*:

Who, if I were to cry out, would hear me among the angelic orders?

Surely, I felt, his eyes had been lifted at the end, and his cry had been heard.

At the funeral parlor I stared down at the closed casket. Of solid

Unnatural Death: Confessions of a Medical Examiner, by Michael M. Baden, M.D., with Judith Adler Hennessee (New York: Ballantine Books, 1989).

walnut, it was selected for its elegant simplicity. Of Jewish Orthodox design, it contained no metal parts, and hence had no handles. On its top rested a small laurel wreath, a woodcut of a religious scene, and a large wooden cross.

How far this heavy walnut enclosure was from the white sack which Tom had always told his friends that he had wanted on his death to be sewn up in and dropped overboard at sea as close as possible to where Hart Crane had given himself up to the Caribbean. The playwright, talking to Dick Cavett on PBS, had remarked, "Personally I want to be buried at sea. I want to be put in a sack and dropped overboard." This same wish is expressed by Blanche in *A Streetcar Named Desire*:

> I'll be buried at sea sewn up in a sack and dropped over-
> board—at noon—and into an ocean as blue as my first lover's
> eyes.

As I stood there and remembered hearing Tom laugh as he expressed himself several times in the 1930s shortly after he discovered the work of Hart Crane, these lines of Crane's returned to me:

> Bind us in time, O Seasons clear, and awe.
> O minstrel galleons of Carib fire,
> Bequeath us to no earthly shore until
> Is answered in the vortex of our grave
> The seal's wide spindrift gaze toward paradise.

I had heard that final line recited with great force and resonance by a drunken Dylan Thomas, one of Tom's favorite poets as well as mine, in South Leigh, on the edge of Oxford in 1947. Dylan's voice, unlike any other I had heard before or since, kept ringing in my ears.

I suddenly realized why that voice was ringing out so loud and clear. It was to remind me that I had witnessed at sea exactly the kind of burial that Tom Williams had pictured for himself. It was in July 1945 at the end of World War II in Europe on the French frigate *La Grandière*, on which in February 1944 I had embarked in Casablanca as American liaison officer. After a half-year of duty attached to the American South Pacific fleet, the ship was returning to the French port of Brest and was planning to drop me off in Panama, along with my liaison party of a radioman, a signalman, and a yeoman, who had assisted me with communications, largely in the decoding of messages. We were on the last Pacific leg of the journey, having left the islands of Nukuhiva and Hivaoa in the Marquesas Islands, which were still in the possession of the French, several nights before, when one night we had a murder on board. Lecorre, the ship's master carpenter, had been working on a gangplank when Robert, a young reservist seaman, had become enraged because he thought that the carpenter, who was an expert and very much liked by everyone on board, had done a bad job. He followed the carpenter up on deck and knifed him in the back with a kitchen knife while the man was gazing out at sea. The next morning the carpenter was dead and the ship prepared for his burial at sea. At sunset the following evening, with the entire crew lined up on deck and the coast of Panama off in the distance, the body of Lecorre, sewn up in a canvas sack, was ready to be dropped into the deep. The scene took place a few days after *The Glass Menagerie*, with Laurette Taylor in the main role, opened to great acclaim on Broadway and made my thirty-four-year-old classmate rich and famous. I had photographed the scene at the time, and the memory of it returned to me vividly with the sound of bugle taps and the firing of the rifles, saying farewell to a shipmate who would not be returning home to Brittany. I had just come to the conclusion of the scene when a touch at my elbow called me back to the Campbell Funeral Home.

Dakin Williams, Tom's younger brother, whom I had not seen for several years, greeted me warmly. He explained to me that Tom's lawyers had thought at first that he should be buried in Ohio, next to his revered grandfather; but he had overruled them and Tom was to be buried at the Calvary Cemetery in St. Louis, where he would rest next to his mother and near such great historical figures as General Tecumseh Sherman and the explorers Lewis and Clark.[1]

I told Dakin that I had just written to him and I had enclosed several programs of performances of Tom's plays in the Soviet Union, which I had attended when I was a Fulbright lecturer in Moscow at Moscow State University in 1980 and my wife and I had lived at the university there. The programs had been inscribed to Tom by Vitaly Wulf, his principal Russian translator. Next to Chekhov, Williams had been for several years the most popular playwright in the Soviet Union. Now in 1983 a number of his plays were running in Moscow and other cities, including Novosibirsk in Siberia. I asked Vitaly Wulf how he accounted for Tom's popularity in the Soviet Union, and he answered that because the action of the plays takes place in what, in the eyes of the Soviet authorities, is a decadent society, the performances are permitted and audiences flock to them. The things depicted in the plays do, of course, occur in the Soviet Union, but as long as they are shown to be the accompaniment of a decadent capitalist society, they get past the censors. But recently, with the new regime, I was told that the censors had begun to clamp down in Moscow even on Tennessee Williams. Just before we left, I had seen a spectacular performance of *Sweet Bird of Youth.* The acting in it was superb. The female characters in all Tennessee's plays come through quite well in Russian. But somehow no matter how talented the actor was, the male Slav was incapable of depicting the Southern American male. He is too massive, too wooden. To the American eye, the performances of the men destroy the credibility of the entire play, but not, of course, to the Russians. Because of the success of his plays, by the end of his life Tom had amassed more than one million dollars in royalties and had decided to travel there with his cousin Jane Smith to collect them, but the trip was never taken.

In April 1982 his play *A House Not Meant to Stand* opened in Chicago and ran until the end of May.[2] *Time* magazine called it the best play he had written in a decade, a work "inhabited by a rich collection of scarred characters." In June of that year he appeared in Cambridge to accept an honorary degree from Harvard. He was disheveled, in an open sport shirt at the ceremonies. He went with Jane Smith to a festival of his plays in Williamstown, Massachusetts, where he said plaintively, "Give my good-bye to Broadway, my many, many good-byes, for there is a rock there, and it is not one from which water nor violets nor roses spring." At the end of all the performances, according to Maria Tucci, he stood in an immaculate white suit and shook hands with all seventeen actors. Toward the end of July, he took Jane Smith and Peter Hoffman with him, first to London and then on July 24 to the San Domenico Palace Hotel in Taormina, Sicily. He continued to write every morning, and what he wrote was not a long screenplay in collaboration with Hoffman as planned but *The Lingering Hour,* "a violent apocalypse of devastation and universal death." Only draft fragments of *The Lingering Hour* are now known to exist.

"All the volcanoes of the world explode at more or less the same times," he told visiting reporters, "and there are earthquakes and destruction everywhere. Here (i.e., in Sicily), there is Etna and the action is set in the main square at a café with people talking. . . . The first earthquake happens in California. Hollywood first disappears into the sea." The title of his play is the usual translation of the Italian *prima sera*—the first dusk he had described in *The Roman Spring or Mrs. Stone* as the moment "before the lamps go on, when the atmosphere has the exciting blue clarity of the nocturnal scenes in old silent films, a color of water that holds a few drops of ink . . . the amethyst light of *prima sera.*"

In August the three of them were back in New York, and after he met for a last time with Gregory Mosher, he flew again to Key West. In November he was back again in New York to read from his work at the Ninety-Second Street YMHA. This reading at the Kaufman was his last public appearance. Richard Kennedy, an English teacher who regularly attended the readings of poets and dramatists, said that Williams received a most enthusiastic welcome from the audience. His opening remark, with his speech occasionally slurred, was that he had almost forgotten to show up. He seemed very uncomfortable. He read excerpts from unpublished poems and from a short story in progress and after only half an hour abruptly stood up and said, "That's the end of the performance."

Epilogue

On the morning of March 5, 2011, I awoke in Paris with a feeling of great joy and went at once to my desk. The previous evening my wife and I had received special permission to attend the dress rehearsal of the Comédie-Française performance of *Un Tramway Nommé Désir* (*A Streetcar Named Desire*) by Tennessee Williams. Directed by an internationally known American, Lee Breuer, it was the first American play to be performed there in the 333 years of that theater's existence.

I found it absolutely incredible that this was the work of my friend Tom (Thomas Lanier Williams), whose beginnings, 1935–1940, as poet-playwright I had witnessed at Washington University in St. Louis. I had attended his first full-length play in 1937 and the same year had acted with him in a French Department production of Jean-Baptiste Molière's *Les Fourberies de Scapin*. Little did he dream at the time that seventy-four years later one of his own plays, in a French translation, would appear in this great theater, the "House of Molière" (La Maison de Molière, as the French say), where the great dramatist's chair is displayed in the foyer.

I reviewed in my mind all of the attention that Tom's work was receiving this year in every part of the world in celebration of his centenary.

For me the citation that gives the best summary of his achievement was offered by a fellow Southern writer, Walker Percy, and is completely unknown to the general public. Percy, a medical doctor as well as a prize-winning novelist, had written this citation in 1976 when Tom was elected a member of the American Academy of Arts and Letters:

Tragedians since Aeschylus have rescued meaning from not-meaning, sense from the senseless flux of time. To Tennessee Williams we owe a special debt. In a tragic age, he has transformed loneliness by naming it for us, suffered sordidness with beauty, graced poor hurt lives with love and pity.

It is to this special debt, here set down so clearly and thoroughly, that I have attempted to bring, in these pages, my record of understanding over many years as a witness.

Acknowledgments

This book owes everything to Thomas Keith, who over the last ten years has worked long hours with editorial precision at New Directions to carry out the wishes of James Laughlin with the publication of the many volumes of plays, poetry, and essays of Tennessee Williams that have reached a worldwide audience. He suggested that I write for Williams's centenary an account not just of his beginnings in St. Louis but of the entire life of this writer with whom I had much in common and to whom I might bring a particular poetic appreciation. I was pleased and honored by his suggestion, but wondered if I had not already said all I had to say. When I began to write, every item, event, or observation recorded led on to another of equal importance, and I was soon confronting, as Tom had, that enemy of all writers, Time. In my struggle with this indomitable adversary, Thomas Keith was of great assistance, and if in the end I have been able to present something of substance and value, I am deeply indebted to him.

I began writing about Tennessee Williams sixty-five years ago and hence it would be impossible for me to express my gratitude to all of the many people over these many years who have assisted me, in one way or another, in putting this book together. I will try to name at least a few of them.

My greatest debt is to the poet Clark Mills (Clark Mills McBurney), who introduced me to Tennessee Williams (then Thomas Lanier Williams) in 1935 at Washington University in St. Louis. As Tom Williams's mentor and mine, I saw him regularly until he left to teach at Cornell in 1940 and I left in 1941 to serve four years in the U.S. Navy. I saw him many times after we both returned from the war, first when he was teaching at Hunter College in New York and later after he retired. We spoke always at length of Tennessee Williams, and I kept notes of those conversations. After his death I spent some time with his widow, Remy, but lost touch with her after she returned to her native Philippines. I have carefully examined Clark's books and manuscripts that she deposited with the Special Collections of the Washington University Libraries and have discovered the remarkable poem, which he had spoken of, and which the library has granted me permission to publish here for the first time.

When I began to work on this book, I was disappointed to find that Dakin Williams, the brother of Tennessee, had died. I had seen him often during his life, and each time he recalled with pleasure the summer picnics that his brother, he, and I had enjoyed on the banks of the Meramec River, south of St. Louis. I have written here of our last meeting at the Frank E. Campbell Funeral Home on Madison Avenue in New York three days after his brother's death. Years later, I spoke several times with his daughter, Anne Caserta, who kindly provided interesting details of the burial of Tennessee Williams in St. Louis.

Of the Williams scholars, I owe most to the late Lyle Leverich, who produced the first indispensable Williams biography, *Tom: The Unknown Tennessee Williams*. I helped him in a small way when he was preparing, as Tennessee had requested, "to report, in truth, his cause aright." I have added a few details that I forgot to mention to him, but he paid me back a thousand times with his book, to which I am deeply indebted, as I hope I have made clear.

Allean Hale, whom I met in New Orleans in 2004, encouraged me to continue to put down my memories of Tennessee and St. Louis in the 1930s and 1940s. We have spoken numerous times since then, and I find that she, more than anyone, has written well and truthfully about his life in that city, which she knew at the time as well as I did. I am extremely grateful for her work and for her allowing me to quote from it. Robert Bray, who read the first drafts of a few of these chapters, made some valuable suggestions, which I very much appreciated. I wish also to thank John Bak, who has invited me to be one of the keynote speakers at his centenary celebration, "Tennessee Williams in Europe," at the Université Nancy 2, France, June 23–25, 2011. I'm also grateful to Albert J. Devlin, with whom I've previously been in touch, for allowing me to quote from the 1960 Edward R. Murrow "Interview with Tennessee Williams, Yukio Mishima, and Dylis Powell," in his *Conversations with Tennessee Williams*, published by the University Press of Mississippi in 1986.

I am particularly indebted to Professor Annette Saddik for her brilliant presentation of Tennessee Williams's belief that what Virginia Woolf (referencing Coleridge) called "an androgynous mind" and Michel Faucault referred to as a "hermaphroditism of the soul" was actually an asset to the creative process. She presents this in her article, "Recovering 'Moral and Sexual Chaos' in Tennessee Williams's *Clothes for a Summer Hotel*," in the *North Carolina Literary Review* 18 (2009): 53–65.

I am especially grateful to David Kaplan, curator of the Provincetown, Massachusetts, Tennessee Williams Festival, and to its director, Jef Hall-Flavin, for all the trouble they both took to arrange for me to speak on September 26, 2010, at their annual event, the theme of which was "Under the Influence" (the worldwide influence of Tennessee Williams). David Kaplan asked permission to use a segment of this book dealing with the playwright's beginnings in St. Louis in the anthology he has compiled, *Tenn at One Hundred*, which appeared in April 2011, with contributions by all the leading writers on Williams. My book has benefitted greatly from the hours spent working on this segment with Kaplan, and I wish to thank him for the attention he gave to every word of my text.

I've also benefitted from working closely in a similar fashion on another segment of this book with Professor John Irwin, not a Williams scholar but an authority on Hart Crane, Williams's favorite poet, and chairman of the writing seminars at The Johns Hopkins University as well as for years my poetry editor at The Johns Hopkins University Press. This segment appeared in the April 2011 issue of the *Hopkins Review*, which John Irwin also edits.

I am grateful to John Irwin also for the photographs of the tombstones of Tennessee Williams and Rose Williams that appeared in this segment and to David Cronin for taking the photographs. John Irwin also put the Press in touch with the archivist of Johns Hopkins University, James Stimpert, whom I wish to thank for permission to use the photograph of Sidney Lanier.

To Professor W. Kenneth Holditch of New Orleans, the Southern writer who best captures the spirit of the poet-playwright, I am particularly grateful. His essay "Acts of Grace," describing the opening of *The Night of the Iguana* in Chicago, December 1961, on the verge of a blizzard, is one of the most moving pieces ever written on Williams. I have returned to it often, as I have to Holditch himself, for the unique understanding and guidance that he always cheerfully offers.

I wish to convey my special gratitude to the playwright Jean-Claude van Itallie for providing details concerning the performance of his play *America Hurrah*, which I saw in New York in 1966 with Tennessee Williams, and for van Itallie's kindness in securing the unusual photograph from it that appears in this book.

Libraries are of supreme importance to writers and I had some of the best libraries I can think of ready to offer immediate assistance: The Bryant Free Library of Cummington, Massachusetts, and its director, Mark DeMaranville, ordered the books I needed from all the other New England libraries. I had a special connection with the Beineke Library at Yale, Nancy Kuhl, in charge of poetry, who sent me a copy of the 1950 letter from Tennessee Williams to my former wife, Barbara Howes, in which he praised both her work and mine. My most important connection is with the Libraries of Washington University, my Alma Mater, because they hold the most complete collection of my work in the country. Shirley K. Baker, the librarian, and Anne Posega, head of the Special Collections, have been very helpful in providing quickly and easily copies of the material they have of Tennessee Williams and Clark Mills McBurney. The curator of Special Collections there, John Hodge, worked with me closely for years on an exhibition for my ninetieth birthday, and later on every detail of this book. He always sent copies of the material he found for me as if any work involved was for him pure joy. It was a terrible tragedy for me to learn that he died in December. No replacement will ever be found who will equal his wit and his understanding. Kitty Drescher was, with her late husband John, my other most important contact in St. Louis over the past few years. Timothy D. Murray, now curator at the University of Delaware Library and former curator of the Washington University Special Collections, kindly sent me a copy of *Ave Atque Vale!*, the memorial tribute of Richard Freeman Leavitt, on Tennessee Williams's death. I was distressed to learn of Leavitt's own death later. He was the author of *The World of Tennessee Williams*, which he had inscribed for me and which I consulted frequently, especially to review the excellent photographs he had assembled. I also called on Joan Ruelle of the Windham Robertson Library of Hollins University, where I had taught, and she spent many hours locating valuable information for me on the American Theatre in St. Louis and on the appearance there in 1940 of Tallulah Bankhead in *The Little Foxes* by Lillian Hellman and later in the New York production of *The Eagle Has Two Heads* by Jean Cocteau. Paula Frosch, retired reference librarian of the Metropolitan Museum of Art, New York, also helped greatly with the research on Tallulah Bankhead.

Many friends on the eastern coast of the United States gave me assistance for which I'm truly grateful:

Ruth and Marvin Sackner of Miami, Florida, who from the Ruth and Marvin Sackner Archive of Concrete and Visual Poetry have provided the Press with prints of my typewriter drawings of Tallulah Bankhead and Ernest Hemingway which appear in this book;

Virginia Dajani, executive director, Kristen Stevens, executive assistant, and Kathy Kienholz, archivist, of the American Academy of Arts and Letters, New York, for the use of the 1976 citation of Walker Percy;

Ethelyn Atha Chase and Helen Houghton, poets of New York;

Daniel Hoffman, poet of Swarthmore, Pennsylvania, and Rosetta Warren, poet of Jamaica Plains, Massachusetts;

Harold Bloom, critic of New Haven, Connecticut; Robert Bagg, translator, and Mary Bagg, editor, of Worthington, Massachusetts; Margaret Bradham Thornton, of Palm Beach, Florida, editor, with special thanks for the use of the Washington University photograph of the production of Molière's *Les Fourberies de Scapin* in 1937;

Paul Resika, painter, and Dore Ashton, art critic of New York;

Paul Theroux of East Sandwich, Massachusetts, novelist; Elizabeth Spencer, novelist of Chapel Hill, North Carolina; Ward Just, of Vinyardhaven, Massachusetts, novelist; Hillary Masters and Kathleen George, novelists, of Pittsburgh, Pennsylvania; Curtis Harnack, memoirist and novelist of New York.

Tennessee Williams would have been pleased to hear that I showed several of his lyrics to Richard Wilbur, former U.S. poet laureate, and that they met with his approval.

In Paris I have had assistance from the following people and places:

The American Library in Paris: the director, Charles Trueheart; Simone Gallo, collections manager; Kim Lê Minh, reference manager; and Janet Skeslien Charles, programs manager, have all given me valuable attention. And my good friend, the novelist Diane Johnson, chair of the Writers Council, has provided encouragement and advice. In addition Kim Lê Minh assisted me with research and with the final typing of the manuscript.

Frederick Wiseman, my friend, who made one of his great documentary films in 1996, *La Comédie-Française ou l'Amour Joué*, advised me about obtaining permission to attend the performance of Williams's *Un Tramway Nommé Désir*. And my New York painter friend, Marielle Bancou-Segal, who has painted scenery for the Comédie-Française, wrote to Dominique Schmidt, the manager, who arranged for my wife and me to attend the dress rehearsal of the play on March 4, 2011. Laurence Flannery assisted in obtaining tickets for our second attendance of the Comédie-Française production.

Laura Furman, a short-story writer and a member of the American Library's Writers Council, as a resident of Austin, Texas, kindly put me back in touch at the Harry Ransom Humanities Research Center with Cathy Henderson and John R. Payne, whom I met on my first visit there in 1985, and with Linda Briscoe Myers, who is currently in charge of photography and who has granted permission for the Press to use the photograph of Williams, the rights to which it holds.

Bob Gottlieb, of New York, on his annual visit to Paris, where he meets with our Writers Group, made some important suggestions regarding this book and put me in touch with his wife, Maria Tucci, the actress, whom I reached by telephone in New York. She gave me memorable details of Williams's appearance in June 1982 at the festival of his plays in Williamstown, Massachusetts.

To Adrian Pilkington, professor of English, who first helped with research and typing of the manuscript, and Alison Harris, photographer, who helped me with research and typing of the manuscript. I am most grateful.

Walter Biggins, acquisitions editor of the University Press of Mississippi, was my editor for *My Friend Tom*. He has been wonderful to work with. His pertinent and succinct comments, offered in a resonant and reassuring voice, have always sent me off in the right direction. Whatever shape and balance my finished text has owes much to his supervision and careful reading. His assistant Sophia Halkias has been very helpful, as has John Langston, the artistic director, with whom I seem to agree on the photographs selected for the book, and Steven B. Yates, marketing director, with whom I enjoyed working at the University of Arkansas Press on the book of my deceased wife, Barbara Howes.

The typist and editorial assistant in Amherst, Massachusetts, who has been charged with presenting the final typed script to Walter Biggins at the University Press of Mississippi is my friend, Peggy McKinnon. I worked with Peggy years ago on a book of poems and the final script was perfect. This book of prose with all its accompaniments has been more difficult especially because I have had to dictate two-thirds of it from Paris, but with Peggy's wonderful sense of humor I have even enjoyed the dictation that I feared initially.

My immediate family offered far more assistance with this book than any writer has the right to expect. My son, Gregory, drove me from Memphis to New Orleans with intermediate stops in Mississippi and Louisiana, and his Southern wife, Evita, allowed me to take him away for the two weeks required. Marc and his wife, Deborah, were a great help with our mountaintop residence in Cummington, Massachusetts, and with the library there and our doctor's offices in nearby Pittsfield. My granddaughter, Marissa, although pregnant with twins in Brooklyn, New York, ordered all the books I needed and made sure that they reached me quickly; and her husband, David, provided important information about New York, where he works. A cousin, Erika Seamon, put me in touch with George Washington University in Washington, D.C.; and another cousin, Bernadette Pruitt, brought from Texas and Oklahoma unexpected, valuable journalistic and photographic assistance. But it was my wife, Sonja, who supervised all these activities from our Cummington mountaintop and our Paris apartment, did all the driving in Cummington, took all the long bus and Metro trips required in Paris, and, at the same time, mastered the use of the computer, which we thought would be used solely for social life and medical appointments and which instead became, night and day, an indispensable instrument for the completion of this book. Sonja has accepted an entire year of total disruption of life on both sides of the Atlantic while attending to my health, which the difficulties of advanced age have not made easy.

Notes

FOREWORD

1. William Jay Smith, "Prelude," in *Words by the Water* (Baltimore: Johns Hopkins University Press, 2008), 3.

2. William Jay Smith, "The Floor and the Ceiling," in *Laughing Time* (New York: Farrar, Straus and Giroux, 1990), 144–45.

3. William Jay Smith, *The Cherokee Lottery* (Willimatic, CT: Curbstone Press, 2000), 24–25.

4. Dana Gioia, "The Journey of William Jay Smith," rev. of *The Traveller's Tree* and *Army Brat*, http://www.danagioia.net (accessed April 14, 2011); Elizabeth Frank, "The Pleasures of Formal Poetry," rev. of *The World Below the Window*, *The Atlantic Online* September 1998, http://theatlantic.com (accessed April 14, 2011); Harold Bloom, jacket quotation for *The Cherokee Lottery*.

5. William Jay Smith, "Louise Bogan: A Woman's Words," in *The Streaks of the Tulip* (New York: Delacorte Press/Seymour Lawrence, 1972), 38.

6. William Jay Smith, "Eudora Welty and Mushrooms," *Eudora Welty Newsletter* 26.2 (Winter 2002), 1–6; Suzanne Marrs, *Eudora Welty: A Biography* (New York: Harcourt, 2005).

7. William Jay Smith, "Tennessee Williams," in *Dictionary of Literary Biography Documentary Series*, vol. 4 , ed. Matthew J. Bruccoli and Richard Layman (Detroit: Gale, 1983); William Jay Smith, *Army Brat* (New York: Persea Books, 1980). Smith has also published a memoir titled *Dancing in the Garden* (Dover, DE: Bay Oak Publishers, 2008).

8. Tennessee Williams, "The History of a Play (with Parentheses)," in *Plays 1937–1955* (New York: Library of America, 2000), 285.

9. Donald Spoto quotes Williams's acceptance speech at the 1969 ceremonial at the National Institute and American Academy of Arts and Letters in *The Kindness of Strangers: The Life of Tennessee Williams* (New York: DaCapo Press, 1997), 278; Eudora Welty comments on Williams's remarks in a letter to William Maxwell (*What There Is to Say We Have Said: The Correspondence of Eudora Welty and William Maxwell*, ed. Suzanne Marrs [New York: Houghton Mifflin Harcourt, 2011], 257); Spoto quotes the comments of agent Mitch Douglas in *The Kindness of Strangers* (356, 347).

ABBREVIATIONS

NB   Tennessee Williams, *Notebooks*, edited by Margaret Bradham Thornton (New Haven: Yale University Press, 2006).

MEM Tennessee Williams, *Memoirs*, with an introduction by John Waters (New York: New Directions, 2006).

LL   Lyle Leverich, *Tom: The Unknown Tennessee Williams* (New York: Norton, 1995).

CP   *The Collected Poems of Tennessee Williams*, edited by David Roessel and Nicholas Moschovakis (New York: New Directions, 2002).

FG   Tennessee Williams, *Fugitive Kind*, edited and with an introduction by Allean Hale (New York: New Directions, 2001).

OD-LA Tennessee Williams, *Orpheus Descending, Plays, 1957–1980*, edited by Mel Gussow and Kenneth Holditch (New York: The Library of America, 2000).

FOA   Tennessee Williams, *Five O'Clock Angel: Letters of Tennessee Williams to Maria St. Just, 1948–1986*, with commentary by Maria St. Just and preface by Elia Kazan (New York: Alfred A. Knopf, 1990).

SC   Tennessee Williams, *A Streetcar Named Desire*, with an introduction by Arthur Miller (New York: New Directions, 2004).

SP   Donald Spoto, *The Kindness of Strangers: The Life of Tennessee Williams* (New York: DaCapo Press, 1997).

CUR Kenneth Tynan, *Curtains: Selections from the Drama Criticism and Related Writings* (New York: Atheneum, 1961).

EW   Suzanne Marrs, *Eudora Welty: A Biography* (New York: Harcourt, 2005).

CON *Conversations with Tennessee Williams*, edited by Alfred J. Devlin (Jackson: University Press of Mississippi, 1986).

AH   Jean-Claude van Itallie, *America Hurrah and Other Plays*, with an introduction by Bill Coco (New York: Grove Press, 2001).

CSH Tennessee Williams, *Clothes for a Summer Hotel: A Ghost Play* (New York: New Directions, 1983).

CAT Tennessee Williams, *Cat on a Hot Tin Roof*, with an introduction by Edward Albee (New York: New Directions, 2004).

EA   Ronald Hayman, *Tennessee Williams: Everyone Else Is an Audience* (New Haven: Yale University Press, 1993).

PROLOGUE

1. NB, 171.

CHAPTER 1

Thomas Lanier Williams, Washington University: St. Louis, 1935–1940
Entire chapter is based on chapters 3–13 of LL, on which I collaborated initially and to which I have now made several additions. My chapter relates Tennessee Williams's beginnings at the University of Missouri, 1929–1932, and in St. Louis, 1932–1940.

1. MEM, 122.

2. CP, "Valediction," 198.

3. CP, "Singer of Darkness," 180–81.

4. FG, xi-xii.

5. CP, 6–7.

CHAPTER 2

Battle of Angels: Boston, 1940
My account of Theatre Guild failure of the *Battle of Angels* production, less depressing to me than to Tennessee Williams, and my reading afterward to Williams of John Donne's poems in his hotel room to save his sanity.

NOTES

1. FOA, 73.

2. OD-LA, 1, 36–39.

CHAPTER 3

The Glass Menagerie: New York, 1946

My view of the Broadway production of *The Glass Menagerie* with Laurette Taylor; an encounter with Williams, who was checking on the performance; and thoughts about his father's absence from the play.

1. CP, 65.

CHAPTER 4

The Poet, Lyric and Dramatic

The poet-playwright considers himself first and foremost a poet; his strength as a poet is shown here, with special attention to the influence of Sidney Lanier.

1. CP, "Nature's Thanksgiving," 213.

2. CP, "Le coeur a ses raisons," 183.

3. CP, "Under the April Rain," 177.

4. CP, "Dear Silent Ghost," 216.

5. FOA, "A Big Storm," 65–66.

6. CP, "Odyssey," 202–3.

CHAPTER 5

A Streetcar Named Desire: New York, 1947

Concentration is on the poker night with the poker players as the center of the play.

1. SC, xii.

2. SP, 118.

3. SP, 118.

4. SC, xi–xii.

CHAPTER 6

Williams and Frank Merlo: Florence, 1949

Tennessee Williams and Frank Merlo drive from Rome to Florence to visit Smith and his wife, Barbara Howes, 1949. Eudora Welty also comes to visit in 1950 and, while there, discovers that she may be acting out in real life a part similar to that of Maggie the Cat in Williams's play *Cat on a Hot Tin Roof*, which she greatly admired.

1. FOA, 18.

2. FOA, 14.

3. CUR, 262–63. See also "Valentine to Tennessee Williams," CUR, 266–71.

4. EW, 216. "During the good times in Jackson, Eudora continues to think about John Robinson."

CHAPTER 7

With Williams at a Performance of *America Hurrah* by Jean-Claude van Itallie: New York, 1966

Williams and Bill Galvin attend a performance of *America Hurrah* at which they encounter Smith and his wife, Sonja Haussmann. They plan to have a drink together and praise the play but are stopped by a drunken brawl spilling into the street.

1. AH, x.

CHAPTER 8

Reading of Williams at Lynchburg College: Virginia, 1979

My encounters with Tennessee Williams over the years, at colleges, meetings of the American Academy of Arts and Letters, and paths almost crossing in Japan, where we both went to see Yukio Mishima.

1. CON, 69–77. Edward R. Murrow interview with Williams, Yukio Mishima, and Dilys Powell, CBS-TV, 1960. Report on dress rehearsal and later performance of Tennessee Williams's *Streetcar*, directed by Lee Breuer, at Comédie-Française in Paris.

CHAPTER 9

Clothes for a Summer Hotel: New York, March 26, 1980

Discussion in detail of this "ghost play" and the light that it throws on the whole of Tennessee's work.

1. SP, 343.

2. CSH, xi. All quotations are from this edition of the play.

3. CP, 12–13, "The Beanstalk Country."

CHAPTER 10

Award of Medal of Freedom to Williams by President Carter: The White House, June 9, 1980

Sonja and I are guests of Eudora Welty, who, with Williams and Robert Penn Warren, received the Medal of Freedom. Welty's admiring program note to *Cat on a Hot Tin Roof* is here, together with Williams's comments on this, his favorite play.

1. EW, 451.

2. EW, 250.

3. EW, 276.

CHAPTER 11

Death of Tennessee Williams: New York, February 24, 1983

My meeting with Dakin Williams at Frank E. Campbell Funeral Home on February 21, 1983, and a discussion of Tennessee's burial in St. Louis and the burial at sea that he clearly had wanted.

1. CP, 8.

2. SP, 359–60.

Credits

TEXT

Hart Crane, "Voyages II" (excerpt). From *Complete Poems of Hart Crane* by Hart Crane, edited by Marc Simon. Copyright © 1933, 1958, 1966, by Liveright Publishing Corporation. Copyright © 1986 by Marc Simon. Used by permission of Liveright Publishing Corporation.

Gertrude Stein, "Prothalamium." Reprinted by permission of the Estate of Gertrude Stein, through its Literary Executor, Mr. Stanford Gann Jr., of Levin & Gann, P.A.

Tennessee Williams, "Ishtar" (excerpt). Copyright © The University of the South. Reprinted by permission of Georges Borchardt, Inc., for the Estate of Tennessee Williams.

Tennessee Williams, "A Big Storm." Copyright © The University of the South. Reprinted by permission of Georges Borchardt, Inc., for the Estate of Tennessee Williams.

A letter from Tennessee Williams to William Jay Smith, July 18, 1974. Copyright © The University of the South. Reprinted by permission of Georges Borchardt, Inc., for the Estate of Tennessee Williams.

PHOTOS

Tennessee Williams as he was in 1935 when WJS first met him at Washington University in St. Louis. Photography Collection, Harry Ransom Humanities Research Center, The University of Texas at Austin.

Sidney Lanier, around age fifteen, ancestor whom the young Williams greatly resembled. Courtesy of Johns Hopkins University.

Painting of Rose Williams by Florence Ver Steeg, St. Louis, 1937. Tennessee Williams Collection, Rare Book and Manuscript Library, Columbia University.

Clark Mills McBurney, Washington University, St. Louis, 1935. Office of Photographic Services, University Archives, Department of Special Collections, Washington University Libraries.

William Jay Smith, c. 1937, at Washington University, St. Louis. Courtesy of the author.

Typewriter portrait by WJS of Edna St. Vincent Millay, with text, from *Literary Birds* (1957). Courtesy of the Ruth and Marvin Sackner Archive of Concrete and Visual Poetry.

Typewriter portrait by WJS of Tallulah Bankhead, with poem, from *Literary Birds* (1957). Courtesy of the Ruth and Marvin Sackner Archive of Concrete and Visual Poetry.

Typewriter portrait by WJS of Ernest Hemingway, with poem, from *Literary Birds* (1957). Courtesy of the Ruth and Marvin Sackner Archive of Concrete and Visual Poetry.

Scene from the Washington University performance of Molière's *Les Fourberies de Scapin*, April 1937, in which Smith played Scapin and Williams played the old father. Courtesy of Margaret Bradham Thornton.

William Jay Smith in St. Louis, June 1942. Having just been named an ensign in the U.S. Naval Reserve, he was preparing to leave for his first assignment at Pearl Harbor, Hawaii. Courtesy of the author.

Frank Merlo, as he was in 1949, when he drove with Tennessee Williams from Rome to Florence to visit WJS and wife, Barbara Howes. Reprinted by permission of the Estate of Tennessee Williams, represented by the Georges Borchardt Agency.

Frank Merlo and Tennessee Williams, Key West, 1955, in the Buick in which they drove from Rome to Florence in 1949. Reprinted by permission of the Estate of Tennessee Williams, represented by the Georges Borchardt Agency.

Still from Jean-Claude van Itallie's play *America Hurrah*, 1966. Photo by Phil Niblock. Courtesy of Jean-Claude van Itallie.

Tennessee Williams as he was in 1977, when he returned for the first time to Washington University in St. Louis. Office of Photographic Services, People Series, #77-414A-19a, University Archives, Department of Special Collections, Washington University Libraries.

Tennessee Williams at Lynchburg College, Virginia, 1979. Courtesy of Lynchburg College Archives.

Burial at sea of a French sailor, off the coast of Panama, on board the French frigate *La Grandière*, on which WJS served as American liaison officer, June 1945. Courtesy of the author.

Tennessee Williams's tombstone, Calvary Cemetery, St. Louis. Courtesy of David Cronin.

Rose Williams's gravestone, next to her brother's, Calvary Cemetery, St. Louis. Courtesy of David Cronin.

Dakin Williams, Tennessee's brother, and WJS at the Tennessee Williams Festival, New Orleans, March 2004. Courtesy of the author.

Also by William Jay Smith
(A Selection)

Poems of Multimillionnaire by Valery Larbaud
Selected Writings of Jules Laforgue
Collected Translations: Italian, French, Spanish, Portuguese
The Moral Tales of Jules Laforgue
(with Leif Sjöberg) *Agadir* by Artur Lundkvist
(with Leif Sjöberg) *Wild Bouquet: Nature Poems* by Harry Martinson
An Arrow in the Wall: Selected Poetry and Prose of Andrei Voznesensky, edited
by William Jay Smith and F. D. Reeve
Eternal Moment: Selected Poems by Sándor Weöres, translated by William Jay
Smith with Allan Dixon et al.

Index